American Sign Language

A Student Text
Units 10-18

Charlotte Baker-Shenk
Dennis Cokely

Clerc Books
Gallaudet University Press
Washington, D.C.

Clerc Books
An imprint of Gallaudet University Press
Washington, DC 20002

http://gupress.gallaudet.edu
© 1981 by Charlotte Baker and Dennis Cokely. All rights reserved

Originally published 1981 by T.J. Publishers, Inc., Silver Spring, Maryland
Published 1991 by Gallaudet University Press
Printed in the United States of America

14 13 12 11   6 7 8 9 10 11 12

Cover design by Auras Design, Washington, D.C.
Drawings by Frank A. Paul
Photographs by Thomas Klagholz

Photograph of Charlotte Baker-Shenk taken by Viki Kemper.

ISBN 0-930323-87-4

CONTENTS

PREFACE

This text is part of a total, multi-media package designed for the teacher and student of American Sign Language (ASL). Included in this package are two texts for teachers and three texts for students:

American Sign Language: a teacher's resource text on grammar and culture

American Sign Language: a teacher's resource text on curriculum, methods, and evaluation

American Sign Language: a student text (Units 1-9)

American Sign Language: a student text (Units 10-18)

American Sign Language: a student text (Units 19-27)

Also included in this package is a set of five one-hour videotapes which are especially designed to accompany these texts.

As a package, the texts and videotapes provide the teacher with information about the structure of ASL and an interactive approach to teaching the language. They provide the student with carefully prepared ASL dialogues and drills as well as information about the structure of ASL and the Deaf Community.

The videotapes are designed so that there is a one-hour tape for each text. The first tape illustrates all of the examples in the grammar and culture text. The second tape provides a 'live' demonstration of a number of the techniques described in the curriculum, methods, and evaluation text. Each of the final three tapes (one for each student text) not only illustrates the dialogues for a particular text but also provides several ASL stories, poems, and dramatic prose of varying length and difficulty for use in the classroom or language lab.

ACKNOWLEDGEMENTS

It is simply not possible to mention all those individuals whose support and encouragement have made this text possible. Likewise, it would be very difficult to list all those individuals whose own ideas and creativity have influenced this text. However, there are several people we wish to mention by name because of their invaluable assistance in preparing this text:

For their creativity, spontaneity, and hard work in making the videotapes upon which this text is based — Larry Berke, Nathie Couthen, Pat Graybill, Ella Lentz, M.J. Bienvenu, and Gilbert Eastman.

For their patience during long photo sessions and their skill as models of ASL — two native, Deaf Signers: M.J. Bienvenu and Mel Carter, Jr.

For his unique artistic skills, beautiful illustrations, and willingness to keep doing more than what was expected — Frank Allen Paul.

For support, encouragement, and a willingness to "pitch in" and "xerox her brain" — Micky Cokely.

For his "good eye" and many hours spent in producing all of the beautifully clear photographs in this text — Tom Klagholz.

Finally, for typing, re-typing, and more re-typing of various drafts as well as for back rubs, seaweed, greens, and unfailing good cheer during the past two and a half years — Beverly Klayman.

Note To the Teacher:

This text assumes that students are familiar with the information provided in Units 1-9 in this series and possess the ASL skills targeted in those units. This text (Units 10-18) is intended to help your students acquire a higher level of skill in some of the major grammatical features of ASL. Again, each of the nine units focuses on a different grammatical topic in the language. Since this text is part of a three text series, not all aspects of a particular grammatical feature are covered in this text. Rather, these texts form the core of a spiraling curriculum. Thus, the same grammatical topics are covered in each of the three student texts. However, the discussion of each topic becomes more and more complex and detailed as the student progresses on to each higher-level text. There are a total of twenty-seven units (nine units per text) in this series. Each unit focuses on different aspects of the grammar of ASL and the culture of Deaf people.

The format of each unit is described in the section entitled *Note To the Student.* As mentioned in that section, we believe this format allows for a great deal of flexibility. Since you know your own teaching style and how your students learn best, we urge you to use this text in the way you feel is most beneficial. We do recommend that you go through this text at a slower pace than you may be accustomed to. As you look through the text, you will see that there is a lot of information in each unit. Please don't feel that you must go through one unit in each class or each week. We also suggest that you supplement the dialogues and drills with other activities that will reinforce the specific grammatical feature of each unit.

Our aim and hope is that the information provided in each unit will, for the most part, be dealt with by the students on their own time. This will free you to devote more class time toward developing their skills in *using* ASL instead of *talking about* ASL.

The two teacher texts *(Grammar and Culture* and *Curriculum, Methods, and Evaluation)* are an invaluable resource for using these student texts. The *Grammar and Culture* text not only provides a more detailed explanation of each of the grammatical features in the student texts, but it also contains several chapters of vital information that is not covered in these texts. In addition, at the end of each of the grammatical chapters, it contains a more complete transcription of each of the three student-text dialogues which focus on that grammatical topic. The *Curriculum, Methods and Evaluation* text not only explains how to conduct dialogues and drills in the classroom, but also shows you how to develop your own dialogues and drills. In addition, that text contains a large number of activities and exercises which can be used to supplement the dialogues and drills in the student texts.

As you skim through this text one thing should be quite obvious—this is not a vocabulary text. Although there are a large number of *Key Illustrations* and *Supplementary Illustrations*, these do not illustrate every sign that is used in the dialogues. Instead, it is assumed that either your students already know the vocabulary that is not illustrated or that you will provide them with this vocabulary by whatever means you feel is appropriate (use of a reference text, instruction in the classroom, etc.).

One final note: As you may know, variation in a language is the rule rather than the exception. There are always interesting differences in the vocabulary and grammar of different speakers or signers of a language. With this in mind, we have tried to include variations in signs wherever possible so that students will be able to understand a wider variety of ASL Signers. However, due to the limitations of space (and our knowledge), the treatment of sign variation in this text will need your reinforcement and expansion. We ask that you supplement the illustrations found in this text with other variations that you are aware of—especially those used by members of the Deaf Community in your area of the country.

Note To the Student:

Learning a second language is not an easy task. In fact, although learning your first language was probably the easiest thing you've ever done, learning a second language may be among the most difficult things you ever do. Learning a second language (and learning it really well) means learning more than the vocabulary and the grammar of that language. It means learning about the people who use that language—their attitudes, their cultural values, and their way of looking at the world.

Thus, learning American Sign Language as a second language means learning about the group of people who use ASL—the Deaf Community. It means recognizing the Deaf Community as a separate, cultural group with its own set of values, attitudes, and world view. Whatever your personal or professional motivations for wanting to learn ASL, you will find that the more you know about, appreciate, and understand the people who use ASL, the easier it is for you to learn their language.

For most hearing people, learning ASL is quite a different experience than learning a spoken language. First of all, to understand someone who is using ASL, you have to "listen" with your eyes. Most hearing people don't have a lot of experience at this since they have grown up depending mostly on their ears to receive linguistic information. Second, to produce ASL you have to use your eyes, face, hands, and body in ways which are not required by spoken languages. Most hearing people tend to be somewhat inhibited about using their eyes, face, hands, and body for communication. This is especially true for many Americans who have learned that "it is impolite to stare" and who have learned to restrain their body movements in order to be more socially acceptable.

Another important difference is that ASL is not a written language. This means that there are no newspapers, magazines, books, etc., written in ASL. Because ASL does not have a written form, we generally have to use English to write about ASL. This means using English words (called "glosses") when trying to translate the meaning of ASL signs and for trying to write down ASL sentences.

Although this is unavoidable at the present time, it has often led people to the mistaken notions that ASL is "bad English" or "broken English" because the grammar doesn't look like English—yet the "words" (signs) are written with English glosses. A real problem! Unfortunately, using English glosses for ASL signs also often leads students to think that ASL is very much like English, when, in fact, it is very different in many important ways.

Remember, the key to successfully learning any second language is: *accept the language on its own terms with an open mind.* If you have an open mind and an accepting attitude, and if you give yourself time, you will learn ASL. Of course, if you are trying to learn ASL (or any language), the most helpful thing is to communicate as frequently as possible with people who use ASL. While no book can substitute for real, live, human interaction, this text provides you with what we feel is a valuable supplement—carefully developed dialogues which are examples of how Deaf people actually communicate using ASL.

This text (part of a series of three student texts), contains nine units. Each of these units focuses on a topic relating to the grammar of ASL and on some cultural aspect of the Deaf Community. The format for each of these units is as follows:

A. *Synopsis:* A detailed summary of the dialogue in that Unit.

B. *Cultural Information:* An explanation of the cultural topic which the dialogue focuses on.

C. *Dialogue:* A presentation of the dialogue with the two Signers' parts on separate pages.

D. *Key Illustrations:* Drawings of signs which have been specially prepared for the dialogue so that the face, hands, and body are exactly as they appear in the dialogue. (We have tried to use the best possible angle in all illustrations for presenting both the manual and non-manual aspects of each sign.)

E. *Supplementary Illustration:* Additional drawings of signs that appear in the dialogue. However, the face or body may be slightly different than the way the signs are used in the dialogue.

F. *General Discussion:* An explanation of the specific grammatical features of ASL which the dialogue focuses on.

G. *Text Analysis:* A line-by-line analysis and discussion of parts of the dialogue.

H. *Sample Drills:* Three drills which provide an opportunity to practice the specific grammatical features described in that Unit.

I. *Video Notes:* A discussion of some of the important things that are shown in the videotaped version of the dialogue (taken from the videotape designed to accompany this text).

We believe that this format allows you, the student, a great deal of flexibility in using this text. You probably know how you learn best and what you need to help you learn. If you find that this sequence does not best suit your needs, then we encourage you and your teacher to take the sections in the order you find most helpful. For example, you may choose to read the *Dialogue* first and then the *Synopsis* and *Text Analysis*. The point is that you should be actively involved in deciding how to work with the text—and not be controlled by it. Use it in whatever way will best help you learn ASL.

Finally, as you learn ASL, remember that it is the language of a unique cultural group of people. Whenever appropriate, try to improve your skills by interacting with members of that cultural group. Don't be afraid of making mistakes, but learn from your mistakes. And don't overlook your successes; learn from them too. We hope this text will help you not only develop skills in ASL, but also develop an appreciation and respect for the Deaf Community.

Transcription Symbols

In order to understand the dialogues and drills in this text, you will need to read through the following pages very carefully. These pages describe and illustrate the transcription symbols that are used in this text.

You can imagine how difficult it is to "write ASL". To date, there is no standard way of writing ASL sentences. We have tried to develop a transcription system which clearly shows how much information is given in an ASL sentence. Although we have tried to keep this transcription system as simple as possible, it may still seem complex at first. However, with patience and practice, it will become fairly easy to use.

The chart on the following pages lists thirty symbols, with examples and illustrations of how each symbol is used. To read this chart, you should first look at the illustrations of signs and the symbols used to describe them on the left-hand page, and then read through the explanation of each symbol on the right-hand page. The symbols found on these pages describe what the *hands* are doing. (In the parenthesis following the description, we have indicated the first unit in which each symbol appears.) Throughout the text in the *General Discussion* sections, symbols will be introduced which describe what the *eyes, face, head,* and *body* do. The non-manual signals which appeared in Units 1-9 are listed at the end of this section.

ILLUSTRATIONS

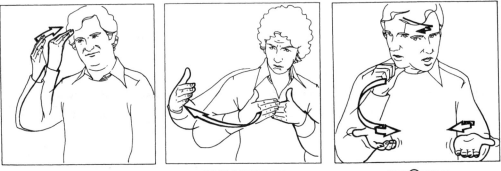

KNOW FROM-NOW-ON NOT HERE

#WHAT DIFFERENT+++ BORED*

TRANSCRIPTION SYMBOLS

Symbol	Example	Explanation
CAPITAL LETTERS	KNOW	An English word in capital letters represents an ASL sign; this word is called a *gloss*. (Unit 1)
-	FROM-NOW-ON	When more than one English word is needed to gloss an ASL sign, the English words are separated by a hyphen. (Unit 1)
△	△	A triangle with a letter inside is used to indicate a name sign. (Unit 1)
-	P-A-T	When an English word is fingerspelled, the letters in the word are separated by a hyphen. (Unit 2)
⌒	NOT‿HERE	When two glosses are joined by these curved lines, it indicates that two signs are used in combination. Generally when this happens, there is a change in one or both of the signs so that the combination looks like a single sign. (Unit 1)
#	#WHAT	When this symbol is written before a gloss, it indicates the sign is a fingerspelled loan sign. (Unit 1)
+	DIFFERENT+++	When a plus sign follows a gloss, this indicates that the sign is repeated. The number of plus signs following the gloss indicates the number of repetitions— e.g. DIFFERENT+++ indicates the sign is made four times (three repetitions). (Unit 1)
*	BORED*	An asterisk after a gloss indicates the sign is stressed (emphasized). (Unit 2)

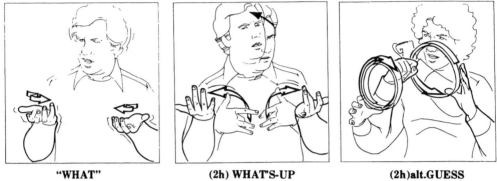

"WHAT"   **(2h) WHAT'S-UP**   **(2h)alt.GUESS**

rt-**ASK-TO**-*lf*   **ASSEMBLE-TO**-*cntr*

Symbol	Example	Explanation
,	**YESTERDAY, ME**	A comma indicates a grammatical break, signaled by a body shift and/or a change in facial expression (and usually a pause). (Unit 1)
" "	**"WHAT"**	Double quotes around a gloss indicate a gesture. (Unit 1)
(2h)	(2h)**WHAT'S-UP**	This symbol for 'two hands' is written before a gloss and means the sign is made with both hands. (Unit 1)
alt.	(2h)alt.**GUESS**	The symbol 'alt.' means that the hands move in an 'alternating' manner. (Unit 5)
rt *lf* *cntr*	*rt*-**ASK-TO**-*lf* **ASSEMBLE-TO**-*cntr*	The symbol *'rt'* stands for 'right'; *'lf'* for 'left'; and *'cntr'* for 'center'. When a sign is made *in* or *toward* a particular location in space, that place or direction is indicated after the gloss. When a symbol like *'rt'* is written before a gloss, it indicates the location where the sign began. So *rt*-**ASK-TO**-*lf* indicates that the sign moves from right to left. These symbols refer to the Signer's perspective—e.g. *'rt'* means to the Signer's right. The symbol *'cntr'* is only used when that space directly between the Signer and Addressee represents a particular referent (person, place, or thing). If none of these symbols appear, the sign is produced in neutral space. (Unit 1)

pat*-ASK-TO-*lee

me*-CAMERA-RECORD-*arc

me*-SHOW-*arc-lf

3-CL

L:-CL

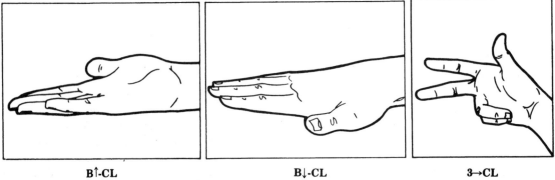

B↑-CL **B↓-CL** **3→CL**

xviii

Symbol	Example	Explanation
lower case words	*pat*-**ASK-TO**-*lee*	Italicized words that are connected (via hyphens) to the gloss for a verb can also indicate the location where the verb began or ended. For example, if 'Pat' has been given a spatial location on the right, and 'Lee' is on the left, then the sign *pat*-**ASK-TO**-*lee* will move from right to left. These specific words are not used until the things they represent have been given a spatial location. These specific words are used in place of directions like 'rt' or 'lf'. (Unit 1)
arc	*me*-**CAMERA-RECORD**-*arc* *me*-**SHOW**-*arc*-*lf*	When a gloss is followed by the symbol 'arc', it means the sign moves in a horizontal arc from one side of the signing space to the other side. If another symbol like *lf* follows the symbol *arc*, it means the arc only includes that part of the signing space. (Unit 3)
-CL	3-CL	This symbol for *classifier* is written after the symbol for the handshape that is used in that classifier. (Unit 5)
:	L:-CL	This symbol indicates that the handshape is 'bent'—as in a 'bent-L' handshape where the index finger is crooked, rather than straight. (Unit 5)
↑	B↑-CL	An arrow pointing upward indicates that the palm is facing upward. (Unit 6)
↓	B↓-CL	An arrow pointing downward indicates that the palm is facing downward. (Unit 5)
→	3→CL	An arrow pointing to the right indicates that the fingers are not facing upwards. This is used to distinguish two sets of classifiers: 3-CL and 3→CL; 1-CL and 1→CL. (Unit 5)

1_{outline}-CL'circular table'

**1-CL'person come up
to me from rt'**

5:↓-CL@*rt*

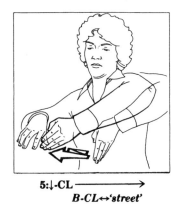

5:↓-CL ⟶
B-CL↔'street'

Symbol	Example	Explanation
outline	1$_{\text{outline}}$-CL'circular table'	This symbol indicates that the hand-shape is used to 'outline' a particular shape. (Unit 5)
' '	1-CL'person come up to me'	Single quotes around a lower case word or words is used to help describe the meaning of a classifier in the context of that sentence. (Unit 5)
@	5:↓-CL@*rt*	This symbol indicates a particular type of movement that is often used when giving something a spatial location. It is characterized by a certain tenseness and a 'hold' at the end of the movement. In this example, the classifier for a large mass is given a spatial location to the Signer's right. (Unit 5)
CAPITAL LETTERS	**RESTAURANT** *INDEX-lf*	When a sign is made with the non-dominant hand, it is written in italics. When an italicized gloss is written under another gloss, it means both hands make separate signs at the same time. In this example, the dominant hand makes the sign **RESTAURANT** while the non-dominant hand points to the left. (Unit 1)
⟶	5:↓-CL ⟶ *B-CL↔'street'*	An arrow proceeding from a gloss means that the handshape of that sign is held in its location during the time period shown by the arrow. In this example, the dominant hand 'holds' the 5:↓ classifier in its location while the non-dominant hand indicates a 'street' with the 'B' hand-shape classifier. The symbol ↔ means that the 'B' handshape moves back and forth. (Unit 3)

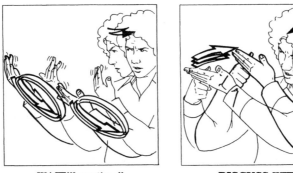

WAIT *"long time"*   **DISCUSS-WITH**
                               "each other" +"regularly"

$$\overline{}^{\,q}$$
RIGHT

Symbol	Example	Explanation
" "	"open window"	Double quotes around a word or words in lower case indicate a mimed action. (Unit 9)
" "	**WAIT**"*long time*"	Double quotes around an italicized word or words in lower case after a gloss indicates that a specific movement is added to that sign. The word or words inside the quotes is the name for that specific movement. (Unit 8)
" "+" "	**DISCUSS-WITH** "*each other*"+"*regularly*"	When a plus sign joins two or more specific movements, it means those movements occur simultaneously with that sign. (Unit 8)
———	$\overline{\text{RIGHT}}^{\text{q}}$	A line on top of a gloss or glosses means that a certain non-manual (eyes, face, head, body) signal occurs during the time period shown by the line. At the end of the line, there is a letter(s) which indicates what the non-manual signal is. For example, '*q*' represents the signal for a 'yes-no' question. (Unit 1)
( )	(gaze lf) △-*lf*	Words in parentheses on top of a gloss or glosses are used to indicate other movements of the eyes, head, and body. (The word 'gaze' refers to where the Signer looks.) (Unit 1)

SYMBOL	**ILLUSTRATIONS**

q *('yes-no question')*

(These photos also illustrate what is meant by a 'brow raise', often written as *'br raise'* or simply, *'br'*.)

$$\frac{q}{\text{YOU}} \qquad \frac{q}{\text{YOU}}$$

wh-q *('wh-word question')*

(These photos also illustrate what is meant by a 'brow squint', often written as *'br squint'*.)

$$\frac{\text{wh-q}}{\text{WHO}} \qquad \frac{\text{wh-q}}{\text{WHICH}}$$

$$\frac{\text{wh-q}}{\text{WHERE}}$$

neg *('negation')*

(Signal includes head-shaking, not visible in photographs)

<u>neg</u>
NOT

<u>neg</u>
ME

<u>neg</u>
FEEL

<u>neg</u>
FEEL

t *('topic')*

$\overline{\text{MORNING}}^{\;t}$ $\overline{\text{PAPER}}^{\;t}$

Notice the difference
between the *'t'* signal
and the *'q'* signal in the
two photos on the right.

$\overline{\text{PAPER}}^{\;t}$ $\overline{\text{PAPER}}^{\;q}$

AN INTRODUCTION TO CONVERSATION REGULATORS IN AMERICAN SIGN LANGUAGE

In order to effectively converse in a language, a person must know and be able to use the *conversation regulators* that are employed by speakers of that language. Conversation regulators are specific behaviors that speakers of a language use to signal each other what they want or plan to do during a conversation—e.g. keep talking, interrupt. Most people are not aware that they are using these signals. However, if someone does not respond appropriately to these signals or does not use them correctly, conflicts may arise in which people become uncomfortable or angry with each other.

For example, English speakers use *open inflection* as a conversation regulator. *Open inflection* means that the Speaker keeps his/her vocal pitch level—neither raised nor lowered—at the end of a statement. This signal indicates that the Speaker is not finished talking and wants to continue. Often this signal is accompanied by another signal—the Speaker does not look at the listener (the Addressee).

Now suppose you (a speaker of English) went to a movie last night and want to tell your roommate about it. You say "I went to a great movie last night" and you end your statement with open inflection because you plan to continue talking and to describe what happened in the movie. However, if your roommate then starts talking and says something like "Oh, what was it about?", you will probably feel a little irritated by the "interruption" and respond "I was just about to tell you that". But if you had ended your statement with lowered pitch and a pause, your roommate's question at that point in time would have been appropriate, and you probably would have responded positively because s/he was showing an interest in hearing about the movie!

This example shows how conflicts may arise when people do not understand (or ignore) the conversation regulators used by other speakers of a language—and how important it is for language learners to understand and know how to use these regulators.

Similarly, in order to effectively converse in ASL, you will need to be aware of the conversation regulators that Deaf people use during conversations in ASL. Conflicts can easily arise between Deaf and Hearing participants when they unconsciously use different kinds of regulators and, therefore, do not respond appropriately to each other's signals. For example, many of the regulators used by hearing people involve the voice (e.g. 'clearing your throat' or saying "Uhh . . ." to show you want to begin talking) and, thus, are not effective in conversations with Deaf people. Since Deaf people generally cannot use or respond to the vocal regulators used by hearing people, hearing people need to learn the regulators used by Deaf people—signals geared to vision, rather than sound.

1

Some of the regulators are briefly described in Units 1-18 in the *Text Analysis* and *Video Notes* sections. Most of the specific behaviors that will be described here can be seen on the videotapes accompanying these texts.

There are two sets of conversation regulators—those used by the Signer and those used by the Addressee. Since people 'take turns' during conversations they frequently switch roles back and forth between being the Signer or Addressee and use the regulators that are appropriate for their role. Signers use regulators to signal that they want to:

    (a) begin a conversation

    (b) continue their turn and not be interrupted

    (c) end their turn and show that the Addressee can begin a turn

Addressees use regulators to signal that they:

    (a) will let the Signer begin a conversation

    (b) will remain 'silent' while the Signer continues his/her turn

    (c) understand and are following the Signer

    (d) want to begin a turn

Understanding how Deaf Signers take turns during a conversation requires an awareness of where their eyes are looking and where their hands are located. Unlike conversations between Hearing Speakers, communication between Deaf Signers cannot occur unless the Addressee is looking at the Signer. This fact makes eye gaze the most powerful regulator in signed conversations since it determines when a person can 'speak' and be 'heard'.

The location of the hands is also very important since signs are made in a specific area called the *signing space*. (See illustration below) Moving one's hands toward or

Signing Space

into the signing space (especially the area in front of the body) signals a desire to begin or continue a turn. Moving one's hands away from the signing space or keeping one's hands out of this area signals a desire or willingness to be the Addressee.

How does a Signer begin a conversation? Since a conversation cannot begin until the potential Addressee is looking at the Signer, the Signer must first get the Addressee's attention. The Signer may do this by using one of several *conversation openers ('co')*. If the desired Addressee is close by, the Signer may wave a hand up and down in the direction of the Addressee in order to get his/her attention.

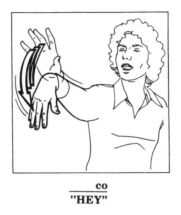

co
"HEY"

Or, if the potential Addressee is close by, the Signer may lightly tap the Addressee on the arm or shoulder and then wait until the Addressee turns to look.

co
"SHOULDER-TAP"

Another strategy is to begin signing with an emotion-related sign which, hopefully, will attract the attention and curiosity of the potential Addressee. Such signs as **AWFUL, WOW,** and **FINEwg** are often used to make the Addressee curious about what is "awful", "terrific", or "super".

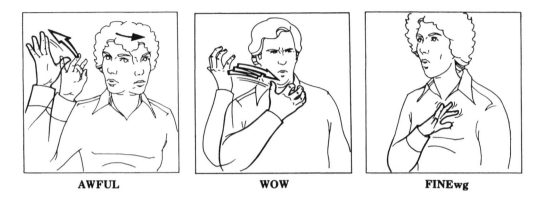

| AWFUL | WOW | FINEwg |

If the desired Addressee is farther away, the Signer may wave his/her hand up-and-down or sideways to attract that person's attention. Or, the Signer may get the attention of someone else near the desired Addressee and that 'third person' will then get the Addressee's attention and point to the Signer so that the Addressee knows who wants to talk with him/her. When there is a group of people seated at a table and the Signer wants to get everyone's attention, s/he may tap or bang on the table so that the vibrations cause everyone to look toward the source of the vibrations. Another way to attract the attention of a group is to flick a light switch on and off several times, or get several people's attention and ask them to help in getting everyone else's attention.

There are several types of errors commonly made by hearing people when attempting to begin a conversation. Sometimes hearing people do not fully understand that it is useless to sign if no one is watching. Thus, they may just begin signing without trying to get the Addressee's attention or may unsuccessfully try to get the Addressee's attention and then begin signing. Either way, no communication takes place, and the hearing person may then feel frustrated and, perhaps, foolish.

Another common error involves the use of inappropriate attention-getting behaviors. Some of these inappropriate behaviors are:

    (a) stamping on the floor

    (b) flicking the lights when you only want to talk to one person and not the whole group

    (c) overly aggressive jabs at the desired Addressee

    (d) waving a hand right in front of the desired Addressee's face

    (e) grabbing the desired Addressee's hands to force him/her to stop signing and to watch

Because hearing people are generally unaccustomed to having to 'work' to get another person's attention (usually just beginning to speak is adequate), they sometimes become impatient when they initially are unsuccessful in getting the other person's attention. Sometimes that person is involved in doing something else, and the Signer may have to wait until the desired Addressee is ready or able to begin watching. It is important to understand that it is more demanding to require someone's visual attention than to require someone's auditory attention. This is because a change in visual attention usually will disrupt any other activities the Addressee may be involved in since most daily activities require visual attention. Hearing students need to become sensitive to this difference.

Once the Signer has successfully attracted the Addressee's attention, the Addressee will generally maintain constant eye gaze toward the Signer (looking at the Signer's face) until they switch roles or something interrupts them. Of course, there is some give-and-take in this "constant eye gaze". For example, if the Addressee is eating, s/he may momentarily look down. At this point, the Signer should pause until the Addressee looks up again. However, in general, the Addressee will maintain constant eye gaze on the Signer's face and will use peripheral vision to 'read' the manual signs.

How does the Signer show that s/he wants to continue signing (without interruption)? Sometimes during a conversation, the Signer may need to pause for a moment to think about what to say next. While the Signer is thinking, s/he obviously does not want to lose the floor. To signal this desire to continue, the Signer will not look at the Addressee (so that the Addressee cannot effectively begin signing) and will keep his/her hands in the signing space in front of the body. The Signer may also hold the last sign made or 'fill' the pause with facial or hand movements that indicate thinking.

How does the Addressee show that s/he is paying attention and that the Signer may continue? It is important that the Addressee give feedback to the Signer which shows how well s/he understands and agrees with what is being signed. To do this, the Addressee will maintain constant eye gaze on the Signer and will use various facial or head movements to indicate how s/he is responding. Occasionally the Addressee may use a sign like **RIGHT, TRUE, WOW,** or **OH-I-SEE** —which will not interrupt the Signer but will show how the Addressee feels about what the Signer just said. Of course, if the Addressee does not understand the Signer or wants more explanation, s/he will ask the Signer to clarify. However, generally the Addressee will keep his/her hands out of the signing space so as not to distract or 'threaten' the Signer that s/he may try to interrupt.

How does the Signer show that s/he is about to finish (or has finished) his/her turn? Generally, the Signer will show that s/he is finishing a signing turn by looking back at the Addressee (so that the Addressee can begin signing) and by moving his/her hands out of the signing space. The Signer may also decrease his/her signing speed. If the Signer wants the Addressee to respond to a question or statement, s/he may use one or more of the following signals:

    (a) lowering the hand(s) with the palm(s) facing up

    (b) pointing to the Addressee with a questioning facial expression

    (c) raising and/or holding the last sign made (if a question has been asked)

    (d) simply looking at the Addressee with a questioning expression

How does the Addressee signal that s/he wants to begin signing? One way that an Addressee shows that s/he wants to begin a turn (i.e. become the Signer) is by moving his/her hands (and possibly head or body) toward or into the signing space. Positioning the hand(s) with the palm up also signals a desire to begin a turn. An Addressee may also point at, touch, or wave a hand at the Signer in order to get the Signer's attention. If the conversation is animated and there is a lot of competition for turns, the Addressee probably will look away from the Signer (as soon as s/he has the Signer's attention) and begin signing. Now the Addressee has become the Signer and 'holds the floor' by not looking at the new Addressee (except to check for feedback). Another aggressive way to 'get the floor' is to start signing, repeating the first few signs until the Signer looks over, and then to immediately look away and continue to sign.

    Again it is important to note that except when joking with good friends, an Addressee should never try to grab the Signer's hands to keep them from signing in order to 'get the floor'. This is quite rude and would be like putting one's hands over a hearing person's mouth.

    Problems with "Mixed" Groups —Problems often arise when several Deaf and Hearing people are interacting in ASL together because they have learned somewhat different sets of conversation regulators. Because these behaviors are fairly unconscious, they are rather hard to control. For example, a Hearing person may use his/her voice to signal a desire to become the Signer (e.g. by saying "Yeah" or "Uh. . ."). This successfully attracts the attention of the other Hearing participants but creates problems for the Deaf participants. Since they cannot hear the vocal signal, they very often miss the beginning of the Hearing person's remarks and may have trouble effectively following the conversation. Often a Deaf person may begin a turn, thinking that s/he has the floor, only to find that a Hearing person has already claimed the floor by using his/her voice. Obviously, in "mixed" groups, it is only appropriate and fair for all participants to use visual signals which are accessible to all participants in the group.

    However, some Deaf people who are accustomed to interacting with Hearing people have learned how to take advantage of vocal signals when competing for the floor! That is, the Deaf person knows that sound will attract the attention of the Hearing people in the group. So, s/he may say something (a word or a sound) which will attract the attention of the Hearing people and then will look away, continuing to sign so that the Hearing people will be forced to stop signing and watch!

    In summary, an awareness of the conversation regulators used by Deaf people is necessary for learning how to effectively participate in a conversation in ASL. Learning how to recognize and comfortably use these regulators will require considerable practice. Students should carefully attend to the written descriptions of conversation openers and addressee feedback in each unit as well as the actual way each conversation regulator is used on the accompanying videotapes, if available.

Unit 10

Sentence Types

A. Synopsis

Pat and Lee are both interested in Sign Language teaching and research, and Pat has just received a brochure about an upcoming meeting on Sign Language. While Pat and Lee are waiting for a friend, Pat asks Lee if s/he went to the meeting in California. Lee says that s/he went to that one but missed the Chicago meeting. Pat says that the Chicago meeting was terrific and says that if Lee missed it, then there's no one to blame but Lee him/herself. Lee knows that but says that s/he was stuck because of his/her job. Pat says that many people went to Chicago, and both the deaf and hearing participants were enthusiastic and excited about it. Lee asks if they were all teachers of ASL. Pat says no — some were teachers, some were researchers, and some were just curious — they were all different. Lee wishes that s/he had gone. Pat says they will print the proceedings and Lee can then read about what happened. Lee says that s/he will definitely buy the book.

B. Cultural Information: The National Symposium on Sign Language Research and Teaching

In the Spring of 1977 (May 30–June 3), an historic meeting took place in Chicago, Illinois — the first National Symposium on Sign Language Research and Teaching (NSSLRT). Organized by the Communicative Skills Program of the National Association of the Deaf, the Symposium sought to bring together Sign Language teachers and researchers so that they could learn from each other and explore ways to help each other more in the future. Papers and workshops were divided into three major categories: Sign Language teaching, Sign Language research, and the utilization of Sign Language research. As the first national conference to focus solely on American Sign Language, this historic Symposium was a time of strong emotions for many people who, for the first time, were seeing Sign Language described as a "real language". Their enthusiasm and excitement led to a second NSSLRT the next year.

The second NSSLRT was held in Coronado, California on October 15–19, 1978. Unlike the first NSSLRT, the second one had a central theme: *American Sign Language and English in a Bilingual and Bicultural Context.* This Symposium was attended by approximately 300 Sign Language teachers and researchers as well as teachers and administrators in schools for deaf children who tried to better understand each other's needs and problems and to share available information from research. A central concern of many of the participants was the widespread use of manual codes for English in schools and programs for deaf children and the exclusion of American Sign Language.

The third NSSLRT was held in Boston, Massachusetts (October 26– 30, 1980) with the theme *Teaching American Sign Language as a Second Language.* Workshops and papers at this Symposium were divided into five major categories: the language and culture of the Deaf Community, curriculum development, teaching methods, teacher and student materials, and evaluation. In addition to experts within the fields of Sign Language teaching and research, experts in the fields of teaching and evaluating spoken languages were invited to share their knowledge and experiences.

The NSSLRT meetings are co-sponsored by the National Association of the Deaf, California State University at Northridge, Gallaudet College, National Technical Institute for the Deaf, Northeastern University, and the Salk Institute for Biological Studies. For further information regarding the NSSLRT and NSSLRT proceedings, write: NAD/NSSLRT, 814 Thayer Avenue, Silver Spring, Md. 20910.

C. Dialogue

Pat

Pat$_1$:
<u>   co   </u>   <u>t</u>
"HEY", KNOW-THAT YOU SIGN⁀LANGUAGE MEETING INDEX-*lf* CALIFORNIA,

<u>   q </u>
YOU (2h)GO-TO-*meeting*

Pat$_2$:   <u>   t </u>   <u>br</u>
"THAT'S-RIGHT", CHICAGO INDEX-*lf*, FINEwg (2h)TERRIFIC, YOU MISS,
     BLAME⁀YOURSELF

Pat$_3$:   <u>(gaze lf   )</u>
"WELL", MANY* PEOPLE FROM-*rt*-ASSEMBLE-TO-*chicago*,

     <u>(body lean rt)   t </u>   <u>nodding</u>
     DEAF, HEARING, INDEX-*arc-lf*, ENTHUSIASTIC EXCITED

Pat$_4$:   <u> neg </u> <u>(gaze lf)</u>   <u>(gaze cntr   )</u>   <u>puff.cheeks</u>
     #NO+, CLASS-*lf* TEACH-*lf*, CLASS-*cntr* STUDY-*cntr* INVESTIGATE-*cntr*,

     <u>(gaze rt)</u>   <u>(body lean rt)</u>   <u>nodding</u>
     CLASS-*rt* "WELL" CURIOUS-*rt*, DIFFERENT+++-*arc*

Pat$_5$:   <u>nodding</u>   <u>nodding</u>
     KNOW-THAT PLAN WILL PRINT BOOK, YOURSELF READ-*book*

Pat$_6$:   <u>   nodding </u>
     "THAT'S-RIGHT"

Lee

Lee₁:
    <u>nodding</u> (gaze rt   )
    YES+++, **CHICAGO-*rt* MEETING, ME MISS**

Lee₂:
               <u>t</u>
    KNOW-THAT, ME, STUCK #JOB

Lee₃:
                           <u>q</u>
    #ALL-*arc-rt* TEACH A-S-L

Lee₄:
    WISH* ME GO-TO-*chicago* WISH

Lee₅:
             <u>t</u>   <u>nodding</u>
    FINE*, BOOK, BUY #WILL ME

D. Key Illustrations

Pat

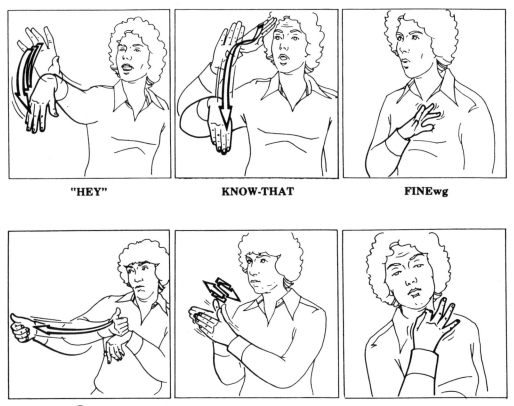

"HEY"   KNOW-THAT   FINEwg

BLAME YOURSELF   ENTHUSIASTIC   CURIOUS

Lee

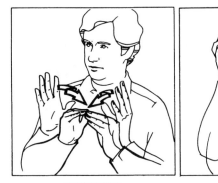  

MEETING	MISS	STUCK

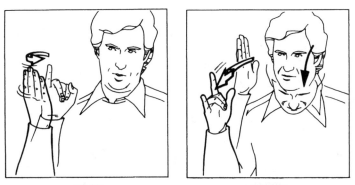

#JOB	#WILL

E. Supplementary Illustrations

GO-TO-*rt*

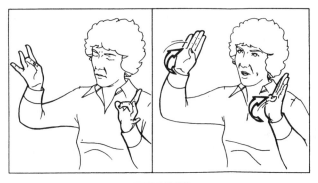

TERRIFIC

ASSEMBLE-TO-*cntr*

DEAF

HEARING

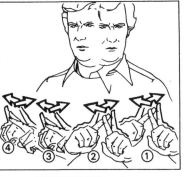

DIFFERENT+++-*arc*

F. General Discussion: Sentence Types

Before reading this section, it will be helpful to review the previous discussion of basic sentence types in ASL (Unit 1). The following discussion will build upon information in that unit. This section assumes that the reader is familiar with the terminology in Unit 1 and can comfortably and accurately comprehend and produce the types of sentences and grammatical signals which occurred in Units 1-9. The discussion of sentence types in Unit 1 focused briefly on 'yes-no' questions, 'wh-word' questions, commands, topics, and negation in ASL. This discussion will provide further information on some of these sentence types as well as introduce rhetorical questions and conditionals.

The previous discussion of 'yes-no' questions described the facial, eye, head, and body behaviors which occur with this type of question. These behaviors can be seen in the two photos below.

<u>   q</u>   <u>   q</u>
YOU   PAPER

Sometimes the only indication that a sentence is a 'yes-no' question is that the Signer uses these non-manual behaviors. In other words, the same manual signs may occur in a statement or a 'yes-no' question; however, the presence of the non-manual signal will indicate whether the sentence is a statement or a 'yes-no' question. (This is similar to the way question intonation is used in English. For example, the phrase 'Pat's here' can be either a statement or a question depending upon the speaker's intonation.)

An additional way of indicating that a sentence is a question is by using a question sign — **QM** or **QM**wg. The sign **QM** often occurs at the end of a question in a more formal context (like a business meeting or a lecture) whereas the variant **QM**wg is used in more informal contexts (like a conversation with a friend).

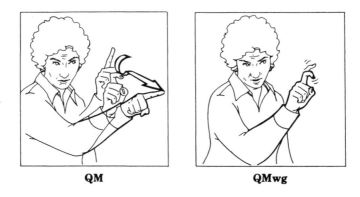

QM   **QM**wg

'Wh-word' questions in ASL have different non-manual behaviors than 'yes-no' questions. Compare the non-manual behaviors in the following illustrations with the previous photos of $\overset{q}{\underline{\textbf{YOU}}}$ and $\overset{q}{\underline{\textbf{PAPER}}}$.

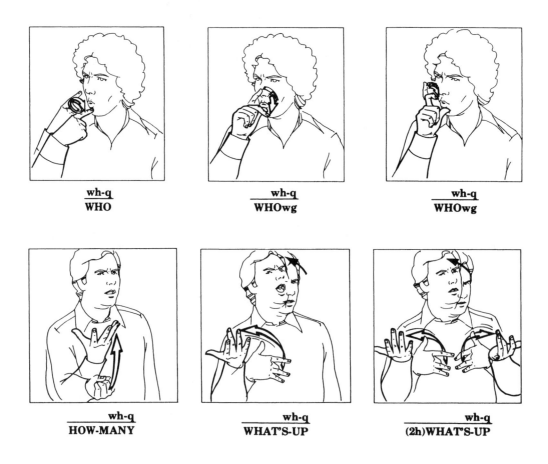

$\overset{\text{wh-q}}{\underline{\textbf{WHO}}}$ $\overset{\text{wh-q}}{\underline{\textbf{WHOwg}}}$ $\overset{\text{wh-q}}{\underline{\textbf{WHOwg}}}$

$\overset{\text{wh-q}}{\underline{\textbf{HOW-MANY}}}$ $\overset{\text{wh-q}}{\underline{\textbf{WHAT'S-UP}}}$ $\overset{\text{wh-q}}{\underline{\textbf{(2h)WHAT'S-UP}}}$

Notice that in the 'wh-word' signs, the Signer's brows are drawn together (and sometimes raised as well). The head is frequently tilted, and sometimes the body shifts forward and the shoulders are raised. When 'wh-word' signs occur at the end of a question (or as the question itself), they are often extended by repeating the movement of the sign. This extension or repetition seems to be a way of emphasizing the question and is seen above in the two forms of **WHO**wg and below in **HOW**wg and the two forms of **WHY**wg.

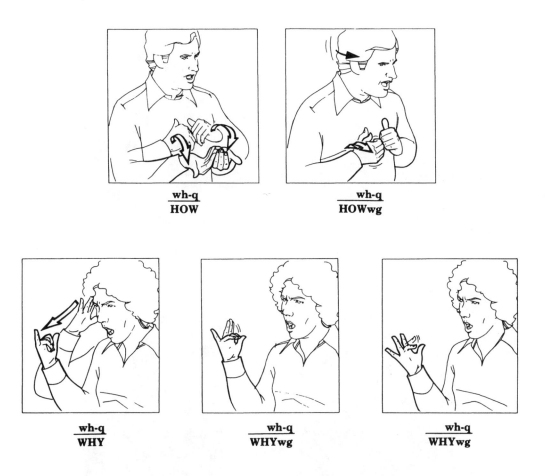

Another type of question in ASL is called a *rhetorical question*. Rhetorical questions are not 'true' questions since the Signer does not expect the other person to respond. Instead, the Signer uses a rhetorical question to introduce and draw attention to the information that s/he will then supply. In effect, the Signer asks a question which s/he will then answer. For example, in English one might say "Mary can't play basketball tomorrow. Why? She just broke her leg". In this series of sentences, the "Why?" is a rhetorical question.

In ASL, a rhetorical question generally consists of a 'wh-word' sign (e.g. **WHY, "WHAT", WHO, HOW**), with or without other signs, and the grammatical signal that we write as *'rhet.q'*. This signal involves a brow raise and, frequently, a tilting of the head. Thus, although both 'wh-word' questions and rhetorical questions usually involve a 'wh-word' sign, they differ in the non-manual behaviors that occur with that sign. Compare the following photos of 'wh-word' signs, paying special attention to differences in the non-manual behaviors.

<u>wh-q</u>
WHERE

<u>rhet.q</u>
HOW

<u>wh-q</u>
WHO

<u>rhet.q</u>
WHO

Rhetorical questions are used fairly frequently in ASL. One of them occurred on the videotape of the Unit 4 dialogue during Pat's last turn. When asked if his/her parents sign, Pat replies:

<pre>
     br   neg   rhet.q   (gaze lf)t
SIGN, (2h)"NO-NO", DOCTOR doctor-TELL-TO-lf,   SIGN,
</pre>

<pre>
doctor-SAY-#NO-TO-lf, IMPORTANT ORAL+ BETTER*, "WELL"
</pre>

Pat uses the rhetorical question (meaning "What did the doctor tell them (my parents)?") as a way of introducing the information that follows—namely, the doctor's comments to the parents about signing.

The rhetorical question illustrated above does not include a 'wh-word' sign. However, many rhetorical questions do include (or consist of) a 'wh-word' sign. For example, suppose you just read an article in the newspaper about a woman who died because she wouldn't eat anything. Turning to your friend, you might say:

<pre>
          co   rhet.q
STRANGE*, WOMAN DIE, WHYwg, REFUSE EAT
</pre>

Or, suppose various members of your club are trying to figure out how to raise money for a project. After fruitless debate, you (the club president) decide to exercise your authority and announce that the club will raise the money by having a carwash.

<pre>
                    rhet.q
MONEY COLLECT HOW, #CLUB TAKE-UP #CAR WASH-car
</pre>

Notice again how the Signer both raises the question and answers it.

Another type of sentence in ASL is called a *conditional*. This type of sentence has two basic parts: a part that states a "condition" and a part that describes the result of that condition. This second part can be a statement, question, or command. For example, the sentence 'If it rains tomorrow, I'll go see a movie' is a conditional. The *condition* is 'If it rains tomorrow', and the *result* is a statement—'I'll go see a movie'. The result could also be a question—'If it rains tomorrow, will you go see a movie?'. Or the result could be a command—'If it rains tomorrow, go see a movie'.

In ASL, the condition is generally signed first and is followed by the result. There are certain non-manual behaviors that accompany the condition—a brow raise, usually with the head tilted in one direction, and sometimes the body leans slightly to one direction. These behaviors make up the *'cond'* signal. After the condition has been signed with these non-manual behaviors, there is a slight pause and a shift in the non-manual behaviors to those behaviors that are appropriate for the result (i.e. whether the result is a 'yes-no' question, command, etc.). The following photos show what the *'cond'* signal looks like and how those non-manual behaviors change in two different result segments. One result is a statement ('If it rains, I'll go'), and the other is a 'yes-no' question ('If it rains, will you go?').

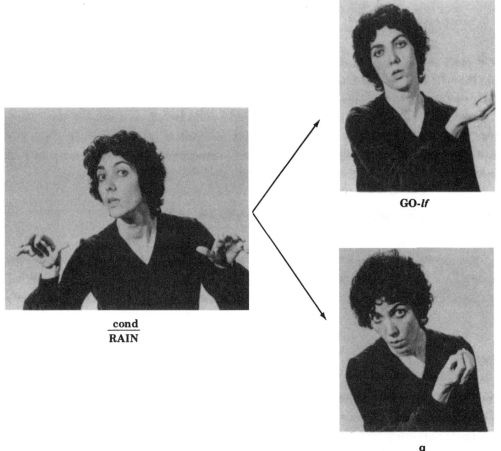

cond
RAIN

GO-*lf*

q
GO-*lf*

Several conditionals appeared in the dialogues for Units 8 and 9, although they were not marked in the text. For example, in Unit 9, Pat$_3$ signs:

cond			wh-q	
SUPPOSE	**POLICE**	**ARREST-***you,*	**#DO-DO**	**YOU**

Pat$_4$ also has a conditional. Notice that the result part begins with a topic.

cond		(gaze rt) t		
SUPPOSE	**HAPPEN,**	**DEAF PEOPLE ALL-OVER U-S,**		

LETTER   *"unspec"people-***SEND-TO-***cntr*   (2h)alt.**COMPLAIN**

Another conditional appeared in Unit 8 (Lee$_3$). The result part of this conditional also begins with a topic.

cond

SUPPOSE   KID   PROBLEM,   "WELL",   TROUBLE   SOMETHING,

(gaze lf)   (gaze lf   )t

"UMMM"   AFTERNOON-*lf*   TEACH AGENT   US-TWO-*lf*,

DISCUSS-WITH*"each other"* + *"regularly"*

Notice that in each of the conditionals above, the condition begins with the sign **SUPPOSE.** This sign or a form of the loan sign **#IF** often occurs with the *'cond'* signal to indicate that the sentence is a conditional. These signs are illustrated below.

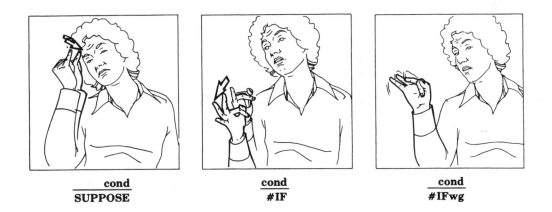

cond	cond	cond
SUPPOSE	**#IF**	**#IFwg**

This discussion has primarily focused on the non-manual signals for 'wh-word', 'yes-no', and rhetorical questions as well as for conditionals. It is important that the reader become comfortable with them before proceeding to further units. Additional information related to sentence types will be provided where needed and where appropriate in future units.

G. Text Analysis

Pat₁:
<u>   co   </u>   t

"HEY", KNOW-THAT YOU SIGN⌢LANGUAGE MEETING INDEX-*lf* CALIFORNIA,

<u>   q </u>

YOU (2h)GO-TO-*meeting*

- <u>   co   </u>
"HEY"

  This is an example of a conversation opener which is used to attract the attention of the other person. Other conversation openers are discussed in previous units and in the introduction to this text.

- **INDEX-*lf***

  This use of indexing has been discussed in Unit 3. Notice that there is 'agreement' between the location assigned to the meeting (the Signer's left) and the direction of movement of the verb **GO-TO-*meeting***.

- **(2h)GO-TO-*meeting***

  This is an example of a sign which can indicate the subject and/or object by means of its direction of movement. (See Units 4 and 13 for further discussion.) Also notice that the non-manual behaviors which occur with this sign indicate that it is part of a 'yes-no' question.

Pat₂:
<u>   t   </u>   <u>   br   </u>

"THAT'S-RIGHT", CHICAGO INDEX-*lf*, FINEwg (2h)TERRIFIC, YOU MISS,

BLAME⌢YOURSELF

- <u>   t   </u>
CHICAGO INDEX-*lf*,

  Notice that the Signer indexes the same location (left) that s/he used earlier for the meeting in California. Generally, the most recent person, place, or thing that is assigned to a particular location will pre-empt (i.e. take over the location of) any other person, place, or thing previously assigned to that location. In this case, the location to Pat's left becomes 'the Chicago meeting' and no longer represents 'the California meeting'.

  This is also an example of a topic in an ASL sentence. Unit 1 described some of the non-manual behaviors which indicate that something is a topic. This type of ordering of information (first indicate the thing to be talked about and then proceed to make some statement, question, etc., about that thing) is called a 'topic-comment' structure. Notice that after the topic has been stated, there is a change in the non-manual behaviors of the Signer.

- **TERRIFIC**

  In the context of sports at Gallaudet College (and perhaps elsewhere), there is another variant of this sign. This variant is used by males, and the one shown in the Supplementary Illustrations is used by females.

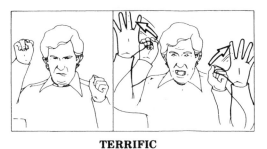

TERRIFIC
(male variant)

		(gaze lf	)
Pat$_3$:	"WELL", MANY* PEOPLE	FROM-*rt*-ASSEMBLE-TO-*chicago*,	

	(body lean rt)		t		nodding
DEAF,	HEARING,	INDEX-*arc-lf,*	ENTHUSIASTIC	EXCITED	

- **MANY***

  This is an example of a stressed sign in ASL. In this case, the sign is produced with a slight hold at the beginning, followed by a sharp, tense release.

- **FROM-*rt*-ASSEMBLE-TO-*chicago***

  Notice that this sign is a plural classifier (5↓wg-**CL**) and that the direction of movement is consistent with the location assigned to the Chicago meeting.

- **INDEX-*arc-lf***

  This is an example of a plural pronoun, as described in Unit 3. Notice that the index is to the left and is consistent with the location assigned to the Chicago meeting.

	q
Lee$_3$:	#ALL-*arc-rt* TEACH A-S-L

- **#ALL-*arc-rt***

  This is another example of a fingerspelled loan sign in ASL. Notice that the sign **#ALL**-*arc-rt* moves in a horizontal arc across the location of the meeting to indicate 'all of the people at the meeting'. This loan sign can also indicate all of the things on a list by moving down in a vertical line; it can indicate all of the people in a hall or auditorium by moving in a horizontal line away from the

Signer. (For this meaning, Signers generally will use both hands.)

                neg (gaze lf)   (gaze cntr   )   puff.cheeks

Pat$_4$: **#NO+, CLASS-***lf* **TEACH-***lf,* **CLASS-***cntr* **STUDY-***cntr* **INVESTIGATE-***cntr,*

  (gaze rt)   (body lean rt)   nodding

  CLASS-*rt* **"WELL"** **CURIOUS-***rt,* **DIFFERENT+++-***arc*

-       neg

  #NO+

  This is another fingerspelled loan. If this sign is produced with a movement from the subject toward the object, it is glossed as _____ -**SAY-#NO-TO-**_____ since it is then used as a directional verb.

  Notice that this sign is produced with the non-manual behaviors for negation which were described in Unit 1.

  (gaze lf)   (gaze cntr)   puff.cheeks

- **CLASS-***lf* **TEACH-***lf,* **CLASS-***cntr* **STUDY-***cntr* **INVESTIGATE-***cntr,*

  (gaze rt)   (body lean rt)

  CLASS-*rt* **"WELL" CURIOUS-***rt,*

  Notice that the Signer has assigned different spatial locations to the three different groups of people who were at the meeting. Notice also that the Signer's eye gaze 'agrees' with these various locations.

  The non-manual behavior referred to as *'puffed cheeks'* is described in Unit 11. One of its meanings is 'a lot' of or 'much'.

-    (body lean rt)

  CURIOUS-*rt*

  Notice that the Signer leans to the right while making this sign to show that it refers to the group on the right. Earlier, the verb _____ -**TEACH-**_____ was made to the left to indicate the group on the left, and the verbs **STUDY-**_____ and **INVESTIGATE-**_____ were made at the center to refer to the center group. However, since the sign **CURIOUS** cannot be moved in space, the Signer instead uses his/her body to more clearly indicate that the sign refers to the group on the right.

- **DIFFERENT+++-***arc*

  Notice that the sign is produced with a horizontal arc, thus indicating that the referent is plural. This sign 'agrees with' the locations which the Signer has just established for the three groups.

H. Sample Drills

1.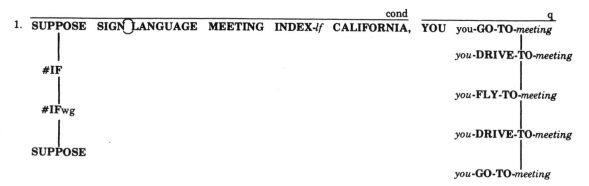

2.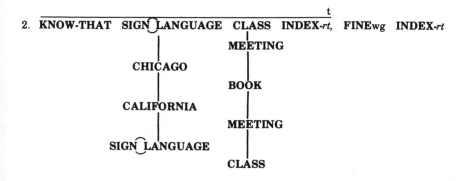

3.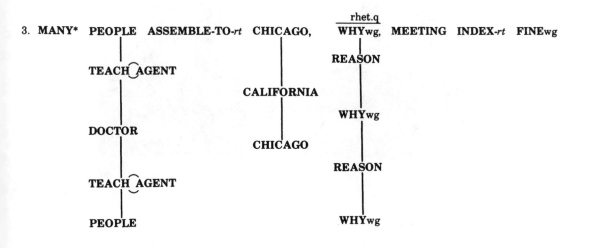

I. Video Notes

If you have access to the videotape package designed to accompany these texts, you will notice the following:

- The clear examples of the following non-manual behaviors: topic (Pat_1, Pat_2), yes-no question (Pat_1, Lee_3), puff.cheeks (Pat_4).

- The stressed form of the signs **MANY, WISH,** and **FINE.**

- The fingerspelled loan signs **#JOB, #ALL,** and **#WILL.** Notice that the fingerspelled loan sign **#ALL** is made in an arc. This can be clearly seen in the 'one-shot' segment of Lee.

- The gestures which are glossed as **"HEY", "THAT'S-RIGHT"** and **"WELL".**

- Some of the grammatical features discussed in Units 1-9: indexing (Pat_1, Pat_2, Pat_3), directional verbs (Pat_1, Pat_3, Lee_4), pluralization (Pat_3, Lee_3, Pat_4).

- In Pat_2, the sign **TERRIFIC** is made with a movement (a flourish?) which does not appear in the illustrations.

- In Pat_5, the sign **READ-**_book_ is accompanied by a particular non-manual signal (an adverb) which conveys the meaning 'casually' or 'normally'. This signal can be seen in the following two photos (showing the sign DRIVE).

Unit 11

Time

A. Synopsis

Pat and Lee are co-workers in an office. They went to a party a couple of weeks ago and now happen to meet during their coffee break. Pat says that the party was really fun. Lee agrees and says that people were talking all night. Pat wishes there was a party every Saturday. Lee says that would be fine—work all week, then party on Saturdays. Pat agrees especially since it would be possible to sleep late the next morning. But Lee gets worried that people would become bored from doing the same thing repeatedly. Pat says that they could do different kinds of things. Lee asks what different things. Pat says just like before—captioned films on Fridays and bowling on Saturdays. Lee remembers and then agrees with Pat.

B. Cultural Information: Captioned Films

On September 2, 1958, a public law (PL 85-905) was signed into effect which authorized the Department of Health, Education, and Welfare to establish a free "lending library" of captioned films for all deaf persons. The primary purposes of this service were: to bring deaf people an understanding and appreciation of films which play an important part in the general and cultural advancement of hearing persons, to enrich the educational and cultural experiences of deaf persons, and to provide wholesome and rewarding experiences for deaf people to share with each other. This program was called the Media Services and Captioned Films Branch (MSCF) of the Bureau of Education for the Handicapped (BEH), U.S. Office of Education.

In April 1974, MSCF became a division within the Bureau of Education for the Handicapped and was renamed the Division of Media Services. The division was established with two branches: the Captioned Films and Telecommunications Branch and the Learning Resources Branch. The Captioned Films and Telecommunications Branch (CFT) is responsible for developing and maintaining the loan service of captioned films to groups which include at least one deaf person. Groups which receive and show captioned films are not allowed to charge an admission price to view the films.

The CFT Branch is not only responsible for acquiring, captioning, producing, and distributing captioned films but is also involved in research, production, and training activities in the area of instructional media. For further information about captioned films, contact: Division of Media Services, 400 Maryland Avenue, S.W., Donohoe Bldg., Corridor 4800, Washington, D.C. 20202.

C. Dialogue

Pat

Pat₁:
<u>   ^{co}   </u> <u>   ^t </u>
TWO-WEEK-PAST SATURDAY PARTY, #FUN* "WOW"++
"UMMM"

Pat₂: YES+, WISH* EVERY-SATURDAY PARTY WISH* ME

Pat₃: "WHY-NOT", <u>(eye squint   )puff.cheeks+cond</u> <u>   ^t</u>
        PARTY*"regularly"* ALL-NIGHT, ONE-DAY-FUTURE MORNING,

OVERSLEEP (2h)CAN (2h)"WELL"

Pat₄:
<u>   ^{nod}   </u>   <u>^{nodding}</u>
    CAN DIFFERENT++-*arc* VARIOUS-THINGS, CAN*
"HOLD-IT"

Pat₅: (2h)"WELL", THINK SAME-AS AWHILE-AGO, <u>   ^t</u> <u>(body lean lf)puff.cheeks</u>
                                                   EVERY-FRIDAY, #CF++-*downward*,

<u>(gaze rt   )t</u>
EVERY-SATURDAY, BOWLING, (2h)"WELL"

Lee

Lee₁:
$$\overline{\text{USE-ASL}^{\textit{"regularly"}}\;\;\text{ALL-NIGHT*}}^{\text{puff.cheeks}}$$
TRUE++

Lee₂:
ALL-WEEK   WORK*"long time"* $\overline{\text{FINISH}}^{\text{br}}$,   SATURDAY   PARTY
FINE+

Lee₃:
$\overline{\text{EVERY-WEEK   FROM-NOW-ON*   PARTY}^{\textit{"regularly"}}\;\;\text{SAME-OLD-THING}^{\textit{"regularly"}},}^{\text{cond}}$
"HOLD-IT"

"WELL", PEOPLE   BORED*   "WELL"
                    "WELL"

Lee₄:
$\overline{\text{DIFFERENT++-}\textit{arc}\;\;\text{(2h)\#WHAT}}^{\text{wh-q}}$

Lee₅:
('trying to remember' _____)q   ('suddenly remembers' _____) nodding
RIGHT+ YOU, REMEMBER ME ONE-YEAR-PASTwg,   TWO-YEAR-PASTwg,   FINE+++

D. Key Illustrations

Pat

"UMMM"

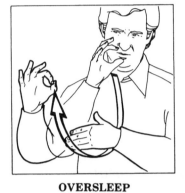

OVERSLEEP

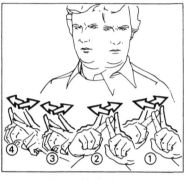

DIFFERENT+++ -*arc*

THINK SAME-AS

Lee

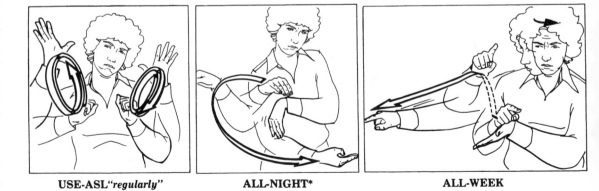

USE-ASL*"regularly"*   ALL-NIGHT*   ALL-WEEK

WORK *"long time"*

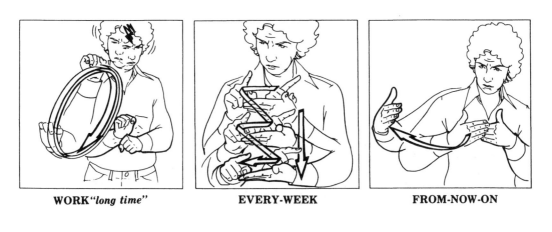

EVERY-WEEK

FROM-NOW-ON

SAME-OLD-THING *"regularly"*

BORED*

REMEMBER

E. Supplementary Illustrations

TWO-WEEK-PAST

VARIOUS-THINGS

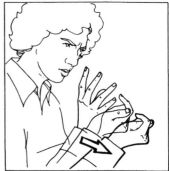

#WHAT

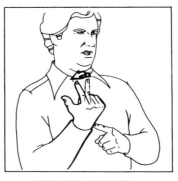

ONE-YEAR-PASTwg

F. General Discussion: Time

The previous discussion of time in Unit 2 provided an introduction to the *time line* and presented signs for various times of the day and for "clock time". It also described how time signs can incorporate numbers and use direction of movement to indicate past or future time. Since the following discussion will build upon that information, it may be helpful to review Unit 2 before proceeding. This discussion will provide further information on some of the features of ASL described in Unit 2 as well as introduce the student to ways that time signs can indicate "regularity", "duration", and "approximate/relative time". Some non-manual signals relating to time will also be described.

The discussion of the *time line* in Unit 2 pointed out that, in general, the direction of movement of a time sign indicates its relation to present time. This can be seen in the two illustrations below. In the sign **UP-TILL-NOW,** the index fingers move from the 'past' into the 'present'; in the sign **FROM-NOW-ON,** the dominant hand moves from the 'present' (represented by the non-dominant hand) forward into the 'future'.

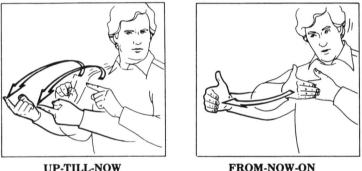

| UP-TILL-NOW | FROM-NOW-ON |

Unit 2 and subsequent units also presented illustrations of how various time signs use direction of movement to indicate past or future occurrence, as seen in the illustrations of **ONE-YEAR-FUTURE** and **ONE-YEAR-PAST** below.

 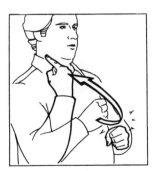

| ONE-YEAR-FUTURE | ONE-YEAR-PAST |

The form of many time signs can also be changed to express the notion of *regularity*. For example, by moving the sign **MONDAY** down in a vertical line while maintaining the same general handshape and orientation of the sign, the Signer expresses the meaning 'every Monday'.

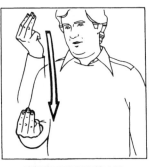

EVERY-MONDAY

For signs like **ONE-WEEK** and **ONE-MONTH,** the regular movement of the sign is repeated several times while moving the sign downwards. It is also possible to incorporate numbers while indicating regularity. This is seen below in the illustration of **EVERY-THREE-WEEK.**

EVERY-(ONE)-WEEK   **EVERY-THREE-WEEK**

There are some signs which do not follow this pattern of downward movement to express regularity. For example, the signs **EVERY-DAY** and **EVERY-YEAR** have repeated, but not downward, movement.

EVERY-DAY   **EVERY-YEAR**

Signs like **EVERY-MORNING, EVERY-AFTERNOON,** and **EVERY-NIGHT** use a horizontal sweep to indicate regularity.

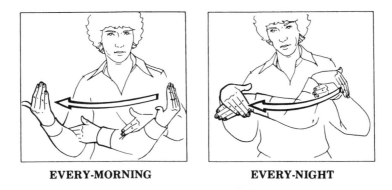

EVERY-MORNING　　　　　　**EVERY-NIGHT**

The form of time signs can also be changed to express the concept of *duration*. Thus, the sign **(ONE)-DAY** or **ONE-MONTH** can be changed to mean 'all day' or 'all month long'. This concept of duration is generally expressed by making the sign with a slower and more tense movement. The Signer's facial expression also indicates the length of time and/or the Signer's feelings about that length of time. Some signs that express duration this way are **ALL-DAY, ALL-WEEK, ALL-YEAR, ALL-MORNING, ALL-AFTERNOON** and **ALL-NIGHT.**

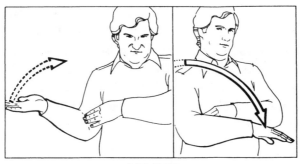

ALL-DAY

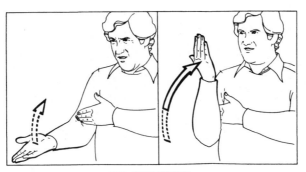

ALL-MORNING

Sometimes a person is unsure of the exact time or length of time of a particular event and, thus, cannot simply use a sign which conveys an exact time or period of time (e.g. **MONDAY, TWO-HOUR**). To express *relative* or *approximate time,* Signers will often use time signs which indicate the boundaries of the time period and then use the sign **THEREABOUTS.**

THEREABOUTS

Thus, if a Signer wants to indicate that someone will arrive on Monday or Tuesday, the Signer may sign **MONDAY TUESDAY THEREABOUTS.** To indicate that something will happen around four o'clock (in English, some speakers would say "four-ish"), the Signer could sign **TIME FOUR THEREABOUTS.**

For certain signs (e.g. **MORNING, AFTERNOON**), this concept of approximate time can be expressed by shaking the dominant hand and forearm up and down. Sometimes the sign **THEREABOUTS** is used after these signs.

SOMETIME-IN-THE-MORNING   **SOMETIME-IN-THE-AFTERNOON**

Facial expressions and other non-manual behaviors can also be used to indicate time in ASL. For example, to indicate that something is close to the present time, Signers use what has been called the 'cs' signal. (This signal can also be used to indicate that something is close to the present space or location.) This signal is made by raising and moving forward the shoulder, and by raising the cheek and side of the mouth toward that shoulder. The larger and more intense these behaviors are, the closer the meaning is to present time. For example, in the illustration below on the right, the Signer is indicating a time that is much closer to the present time (more recent) than the time indicated in the illustration on the left.

| | cs |
| RECENT | RECENT |

The 'cs' signal can also occur with signs like **NOW, ONE-DAY-PAST,** and **ONE-YEAR-PAST** for the purpose of emphasizing their closeness to the present time. For example, in the illustration below on the right, the Signer is expressing the meaning 'just now' or 'right now'.

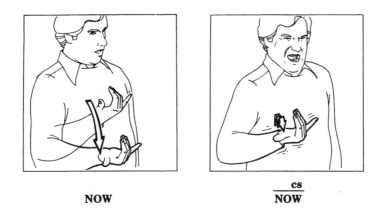

| | cs |
| NOW | NOW |

The *'cs'* signal can also occur with verbs to indicate that something just happened or is soon about to happen. Suppose the Signer wants to indicate that someone has 'just arrived'. In this case, s/he might use the sign **ARRIVE-AT-_____** with the *'cs'* signal.

cs
ARRIVE-AT-*here*

Just as the *'cs'* signal indicates that something is close in time or space, there are facial expressions that Signers frequently use to show that something is far away in time or space. One of these expressions is *'puffed cheeks'* and another is the *'intense'* expression. The meanings conveyed by the *'puff.cheeks'* signal are 'a lot; a huge number of; large; of great magnitude'. The *'intense'* expression conveys the meanings 'awfully large; surprisingly huge; to an unusually great degree'. Thus, when used with a time sign like **DISTANT-FUTURE**, the *'puff.cheeks'* signal conveys the meaning 'far into the future', and the *'intense'* signal conveys the meaning 'awfully far into the future'. (In the illustration below on the right, the dotted lines indicate that the movement was slower during that part of the sign. This illustrates a stressed form of the sign.)

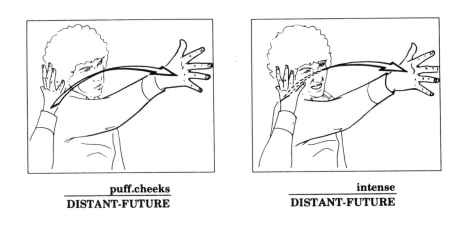

puff.cheeks   **intense**
DISTANT-FUTURE   **DISTANT-FUTURE**

This discussion has focused on ways to express regularity, duration, and approximate time with time signs. Several non-manual signals that can refer to time were also introduced. Further discussion of some of these time signs will occur in subsequent units. However, it is important to become comfortable with the non-manual signals now since they occur quite frequently in ASL with many different types of signs to indicate closeness to or distance from present time or space, as well as relative size, quantity, and intensity.

G. Text Analysis

Pat₁:

$$\overline{\text{co}} \qquad \overline{\text{t}}$$
"UMMM" TWO-WEEK-PAST SATURDAY PARTY, #FUN* "WOW"++

$$\overline{\qquad\qquad\qquad\qquad\qquad\qquad\text{t}}$$
- **TWO-WEEK-PAST SATURDAY PARTY,**

    Notice that this portion of Pat's turn is accompanied by the non-manual behaviors used to indicate a 'topic'. Generally a topic is indicated by raising the brows, tilting the head, and holding the last sign of the phrase slightly longer than usual. See Unit 1 for further discussion.

    Notice also that the sign **TWO-WEEK-PAST** is an example of number incorporation—the handshape used to represent the number '2' is the handshape used in this sign. The sign then moves 'toward the past' in relation to the *time line,* as illustrated in Unit 2.

- **#FUN***

    This is an example of a fingerspelled loan sign. Notice that it is stressed.

Lee₁:

$$\overline{\text{puff.cheeks}}$$
TRUE++ USE-ASL*"regularly" ALL-NIGHT*

$$\overline{\text{puff.cheeks}}$$
- **USE-ASL***"regularly"

    Notice that the Signer uses the verb modulation *"regularly"* which was discussed in Unit 8. Here this modulation conveys the meaning 'a lot'. This meaning is also conveyed by the non-manual signal *'puff.cheeks'*, which was described in the *General Discussion* section.

- **ALL-NIGHT***

    This is an example of a sign whose basic form has been modified to express the idea of duration. For further information, see the *General Discussion* section above.

Pat$_2$:   YES+, WISH* EVERY-SATURDAY PARTY WISH* ME

- **EVERY-SATURDAY**

  This is an example of a sign whose basic form has been modified to indicate regularity. For further information, see the *General Discussion* section above.

$$\overline{}^{br}$$

Lee$_2$:   *FINE+*   ALL-WEEK WORK*"long time"* $\overline{\text{FINISH,}}$ SATURDAY PARTY

- **ALL-WEEK**

  This is another example of a sign whose basic form has been modified to express the additional idea of duration. Notice that the dotted lines in the illustration indicate a tenseness and slowness which is generally characteristic of signs expressing the concept of duration.

- **WORK***"long time"*

  This is an example of one of the verb modulations described in Unit 8. The meaning it conveys is that from the Signer's perspective, the action (**WORK**) happens 'for a long time'.

Pat$_3$: $\overline{\text{(eye squint)puff.cheeks + cond}}$ "WHY-NOT", **PARTY***"regularly"* **ALL-NIGHT,** $\overline{\text{ONE-DAY-FUTURE͡MORNING,}}^{t}$

OVERSLEEP (2h)CAN (2h)"WELL"

- $\overline{\text{(eye squint)puff.cheeks + cond}}$
  PARTY*"regularly"* **ALL-NIGHT,**

  This is an example of the condition portion of a conditional statement in ASL. Notice that the condition is not introduced by a sign (like **SUPPOSE, #IF,** or **#IF**wg); rather the only indication of the condition is the non-manual signal *'cond'*. See Unit 10 for more information.

  Notice also that the Signer uses the verb modulation *"regularly"*. The combination of this modulation with the *'puff.cheeks'* signal and the Signer's eye squint seem to give the meaning 'party without stopping'.

- **ONE-DAY-FUTURE͡MORNING**

  This is an example of two signs which are made in such a way that they seem like a single sign. When these two signs are used in this way, the meaning is 'the next morning' or 'the morning after'.

ee_3:

                                                                               cond

EVERY-WEEK   FROM-NOW-ON*   PARTY"*regularly*"   **SAME-OLD-THING**"*regularly*"

"*HOLD-IT*"

"WELL", PEOPLE BORED* "WELL"
                 "*WELL*"

---

                                                                               cond

• **EVERY-WEEK   FROM-NOW-ON*   PARTY**"*regularly*"   **SAME-OLD-THING**"*regularly*"

> Notice that this condition is signed with no manual signal (e.g. **SUPPOSE, #IF, #IFwg**). See Unit 10 for a description and discussion of the '*cond*' signal.
>
> Notice also that Lee signs **PARTY**"*regularly*" using the same verb modulation that Pat used in the previous turn. This is appropriate since Lee is commenting on the situation Pat has proposed.
>
> Lee also uses the modulation "*regularly*" with the sign **SAME-OLD-THING**, referring to a frequent repetition of the same thing (partying). This sign often occurs with the "*regularly*" modulation, the "*long time*" modulation (see Unit 8), or another modulation referred to as "*over & over again*" (see Unit 17). Again, the choice of which of these movements the Signer uses is dependent upon his/her perceptions of how long or frequently things are the same.

t_4:

                  nod   nodding

       CAN   DIFFERENT++ -*arc*   **VARIOUS-THINGS,   CAN***

"*HOLD-IT*"

> • **DIFFERENT++** -*arc*
>
> This is an example of repeating a sign in an arc to show that the object is plural. Further description of this way of indicating plurality can be found in Units 3, 12, and 16.

t_5:

                                                              t   (body lean lf)puff.cheeks

(2h)"WELL", THINK‿SAME-AS AWHILE-AGO, EVERY-FRIDAY,   # CF++-*downward,*

(gaze rt   )t

EVERY-SATURDAY, BOWLING, (2h)"WELL"

> • **THINK‿SAME-AS**
>
> This is an example of two signs which, when used together, often look like a single sign. When they occur together, the meaning they convey is 'just like', 'just as', or 'it's like'.

- **EVERY-FRIDAY**

  This sign and the sign **EVERY-SATURDAY** are examples of signs that indicate regularity. Notice how the form of the sign is different if the Signer wants to talk about 'every other _____' rather than 'every _____'.

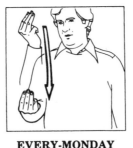

EVERY-MONDAY   EVERY-OTHER-MONDAY

- **#CF++-*downward***

  The fingerspelled loan sign **#CF** is a common way of referring to captioned films. Notice that although **#CF** appears to be an abbreviation, it is different than **S-F** (San Francisco) or **P-A** (Pennsylvania) because these are actual abbreviations in English (S.F. and Pa.) which have been borrowed into ASL. However, C.F. is not a commonly used English abbreviation for captioned films.

				('trying to remember'	)q	('suddenly remembers')	nodding
Lee$_5$:	RIGHT+	YOU,	REMEMBER	ME ONE-YEAR-PASTwg,		TWO-YEAR-PASTwg,	FINE+++

- **ONE-YEAR-PASTwg   TWO-YEAR-PASTwg**

  These two signs are examples of number incorporation with the sign **YEAR**. Notice also that the movement of both signs is 'toward the past'. (See Unit 2 for a discussion of the *time line*.)

  Both of these signs have alternate forms which involve moving the dominant hand 'toward the past' instead of flicking the index finger (or index and middle fingers) 'toward the past'. Compare the following illustrations.

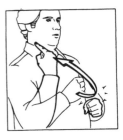

ONE-YEAR-PASTwg   ONE-YEAR-PAST

H. Sample Drills

WISH*   EVERY-SATURDAY   PARTY   WISH*   ME

       EVERY-WEEK

       ALL-DAY

       ALL-WEEK

       ALL-NIGHT

       EVERY-MONTH

       EVERY-YEAR

       EVERY-THREE-MONTH

       EVERY-TWO-YEAR

       EVERY-DAY

       EVERY-MONDAY

       EVERY-SATURDAY

---

                                                                                                        cond

EVERY-WEEK   FROM-NOW-ON*   PARTY*"regularly"*   SAME-OLD-THING*"regularly"*,   PEOPLE   BORED*

EVERY-MONTH

                               # CF+ + -*downward*

ALL-WEEK

                               WORK*"regularly"*

EVERY-DAY

                               PARTY*"regularly"*

EVERY-WEEK

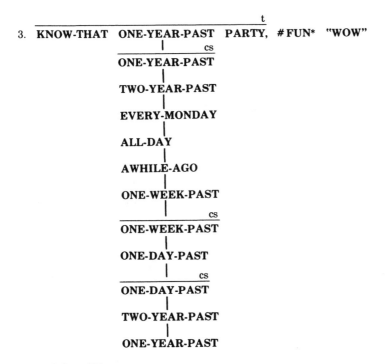

                                          t

3.   **KNOW-THAT ONE-YEAR-PAST PARTY, #FUN* "WOW"**

                    | cs

                  ONE-YEAR-PAST

                  |

                  TWO-YEAR-PAST

                  |

                  EVERY-MONDAY

                  |

                  ALL-DAY

                  |

                  AWHILE-AGO

                  |

                  ONE-WEEK-PAST

                  | cs

                  ONE-WEEK-PAST

                  |

                  ONE-DAY-PAST

                  | cs

                  ONE-DAY-PAST

                  |

                  TWO-YEAR-PAST

                  |

                  ONE-YEAR-PAST

I. Video Notes

If you have access to the videotape package designed to accompany these texts, you will notice the following:

- Examples of several non-manual signals which occur: *'cond'* (Pat$_3$, Lee$_3$), *'puff.cheeks'* (Lee$_1$, Pat$_3$, Pat$_5$), *'wh-q'* (Lee$_4$).

- In Pat's third turn, the combination of the *'puff.cheeks'* signal and the *"regularly"* modulation with the sign **PARTY** seem to convey the meaning 'to party without stopping' or 'party incessantly'.

- In Lee$_3$, the sign **EVERY-WEEK** does not move downward; rather the sign is held in a constant location.

- Also in Lee$_3$, the sign glossed as **BORED*** is different than the sign illustrated above. The sign used on the videotape seems to be more 'intense' or 'forceful' than the sign previously illustrated. It also seems to be more informal than the one illustrated in this unit.

- In Lee$_1$ and Lee$_3$, the signs **ALL-NIGHT*** and **FROM-NOW-ON*** are both stressed. However, the sign **ALL-NIGHT*** is made with a fast, sharp movement while the sign **FROM-NOW-ON*** is made with a slower, more tense movement.

- The type of feedback that the Signers give each other during the other's turn, like head nodding and changes in facial expression. Also notice how Pat signs **THAT-ONE** during Lee's fifth turn.

- In Pat$_5$, the Signer uses the sign **IDEA⌢SAME-AS** instead of **THINK⌢SAME-AS**. Both of these signs express the meaning 'just as', 'it's like', 'sorta like'.

Unit 12
Pronominalization

A. Synopsis

Pat and Lee are both members of the same Deaf club. They are having dinner at a restaurant and Pat asks Lee if s/he is going to the movie tomorrow night. Lee asks if the movie is captioned. Pat says no, it will be interpreted by a woman with short black hair. Lee asks if it's the same one who interprets every morning on T.V. Pat says that's the one and suggests that the two of them go to the movie. Lee says that s/he will stay put; s/he doesn't like looking back and forth between the interpreter and the movie. Pat says that's Lee's decision but Pat and two friends are going. Lee asks if Pat minds interpreted movies. Pat says it doesn't matter, the movie is important—Star Wars! When Lee finds that out, s/he agrees to join Pat and the others.

B. Cultural Information: The Registry of Interpreters for the Deaf

The Registry of Interpreters for the Deaf, Inc. (RID) is a national organization of deaf and hearing individuals who help facilitate communication between deaf and hearing people. The RID was established in 1964 (although from 1964–1965, the name of the organization was The National Registry of Professional Interpreters and Translators for the Deaf). The original purpose of the organization was to maintain a list of qualified interpreters and to encourage the recruiting and training of more interpreters.

In 1964, the organization had only a few members compared with its present membership—over 4000. Most of these 4000 members also belong to one of the sixty (60) local chapter affiliates of the RID. These local chapter affiliates often publish newsletters, host workshops, and sponsor evaluations of individuals who wish to be certified by the RID. Each of these local chapter affiliates has its own president and other elected officers.

The evaluation and certification of interpreters by the RID began in 1972 in order to provide a certain level of quality control within the profession. Since that time, approximately 2000 individuals have been certified at varying levels of competence. Because of the growing demand for interpreting services in educational, legal, medical, and other settings and because of the specialized skills needed to effectively interpret in these settings, the RID has begun to certify individuals in specialty areas. In addition to evaluation and certification, the RID also publishes a variety of materials related to interpreting (e.g. *Regional Directory of Services for Deaf Persons, Resource Guide to Interpreter Training Programs, Introduction to Interpreting*). For further information, contact the RID Home Office: RID, Inc., 814 Thayer Avenue, Silver Spring, Md. 20910.

C. Dialogue

Pat

Pat₁: ONE-DAY-FUTURE‿NIGHT $\overline{\text{MOVIE,}}^{\text{t}}$ $\overline{\text{YOU   GO-TO-}rt}^{\text{q}}$

Pat₂: $\overline{\text{INTERPRET+,}}^{\text{neg}}$ $\overline{\text{KNOW+   WOMAN}}$ $\overline{\text{SMALL-}rt\quad\text{BLACK   H-A-I-R}}^{\text{(gaze rt,pursed lips)}}$ $\overline{\text{THAT-ONE‿INDEX-}rt}^{\text{(rapid nodding   )q}}$

Pat₃: $\overline{\text{RIGHT++,}}^{\text{nodding}}$ $\overline{\text{US-TWO   GO-}rt}^{\text{(gaze rt)}}$ $\overline{\text{WHY‿NOT}}^{\text{wh-q}}$

Pat₄: THINK‿YOURSELF, ⒥ , ⒝ , $\overline{\text{US-THREE,}}^{\text{t}}$ $\overline{\text{GO-}rt}^{\text{nod}}$

Pat₅: $\overline{\text{DOESN'T-MATTER,}}^{\text{neg}}$ MOVIE IMPORTANT*, S-T-A-R-W-A-R-S

Lee

Lee₁:
$$\overline{\text{MOVIE \quad CAPTION \quad QMwg}}^{\text{q}}$$

Lee₂:
$$\overline{}^{\text{nodding}} \quad \text{SAME-AS \quad EVERY-MORNING \quad \#TV} \quad \overline{\text{THAT-ONE INDEX-}lf}^{\text{q}}$$

Lee₃:
$$\overline{}^{\text{neg}} \quad \text{ME \quad (2h)STAY-}here, \quad \text{MOVIE \quad INTERPRET} \quad \overline{me\text{-LOOK-AT-}lf \text{ \& } rt\leftrightarrow}^{\text{(gaze lf \& rt}\leftrightarrow \text{)t}}, \quad \overline{\text{NOT-LIKE*} \quad \text{ME}}^{\text{neg}}$$

Lee₄:
$$\overline{\text{MOVIE \quad INTERPRET \quad DON'T-CARE \quad YOU}}^{\text{q}}$$

Lee₅:
('happily surprised')
S-T-A-R-W-A-R-S,   ME *me*-JOIN-*you** GO-*lf**

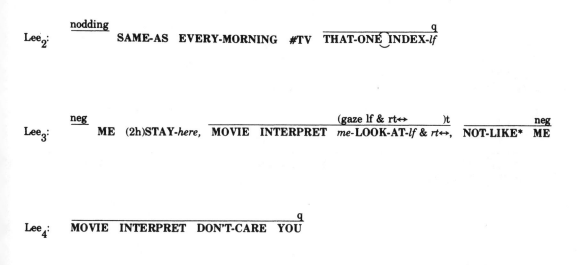

D. Key Illustrations

Pat

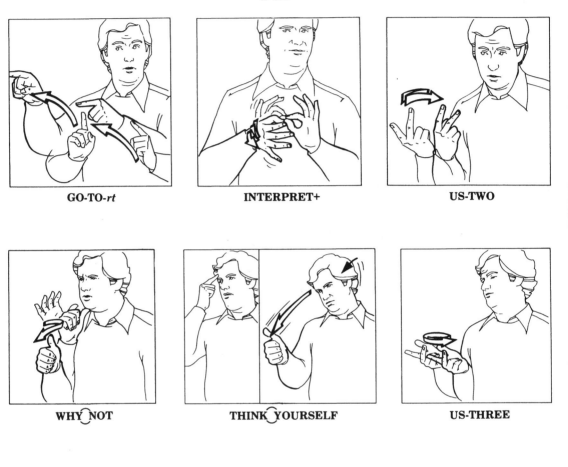

GO-TO-*rt*   INTERPRET+   US-TWO

WHY͡NOT   THINK͡YOURSELF   US-THREE

Lee

CAPTION

QMwg

EVERY-MORNING

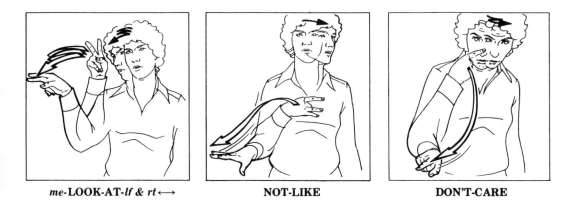

me-LOOK-AT-*lf* & *rt* ⟷   NOT-LIKE   DON'T-CARE

E. Supplementary Illustrations

KNOW+   MOVIE   THAT-ONE INDEX-*rt*

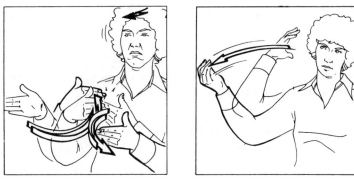

DOESN'T-MATTER   GO-*rt*

F. General Discussion: Pronominalization

Before reading this section, it will be helpful to review the previous discussion of pronominalization in Unit 3. That unit introduced ways to refer to people using the indexic (index finger), honorific, or reflexive/emphatic pronouns. It also presented the *reality principle* and ways to assign specific spatial locations to referents. This unit will expand upon some of these topics and will introduce strategies for referring to three, four, and five people or things, eye indexing, definite reference, and additional ways to set up people, places, or things in space.

As described in Unit 3, pronominal reference generally involves 'pointing' to a person or persons with a particular handshape. The handshape that is used indicates the type of reference. For example, in the four illustrations below notice the similarity between the pronoun on the left and the one on the right. The difference in handshape indicates that the pronouns on the left are indexic (meaning 'we') whereas the ones on the right are reflexive/emphatic (meaning 'ourselves').

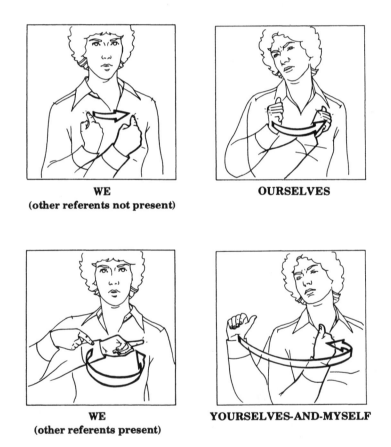

WE	OURSELVES
(other referents not present)	
WE	YOURSELVES-AND-MYSELF
(other referents present)	

Similarly, the handshape made with the hand flat and fingers together is used for possessive reference. When a Signer 'points' with the palm of the hand to him/herself, the meaning is 'my' or 'mine'. When a Signer points with the palm facing the person s/he is talking with, the meaning is 'your' or 'yours'. Pointing to a third person means 'his', 'her', or 'hers'. When the hand moves from one side of the Signer's chest to the other side (as in the first two illustrations above) the meaning is 'our' or 'ours'. If the pronoun refers to more than one person (not including the Signer), the hand will 'sweep' across the spatial locations of those persons. For example, if the Signer is conversing with two friends and wants to ask 'Are *your* parents coming to Graduation Day?', the possessive handshape would move from one friend to the other to express the meaning 'your'.

YOUR (plural)

As discussed in Unit 3, when a Signer wishes to refer to two people together or two things together, s/he will normally use the handshape illustrated on the left or its variant on the right.

By moving either of these handshapes back and forth between the two people or two things, the Signer can express the meanings 'us two', 'you and I', 'you two', 'those two', 's/he and I', etc. Similarly, by using the handshape illustrated below, the Signer can refer to three people or three things. Instead of a back and forth movement, this handshape (palm up) is used with a circular movement made close to the three people or three things the Signer wishes to refer to.

For example, suppose the Signer is talking with three friends—A, B, and C—as pictured below.

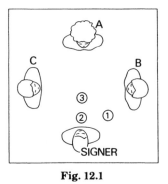

Fig. 12.1

The Signer could use this handshape to express the meanings—'us three' (Signer + B + A), 'us three' (Signer + B + C), or 'you three' (B + A + C), depending on the location of the pronoun (see numbers 1, 2, 3 above).

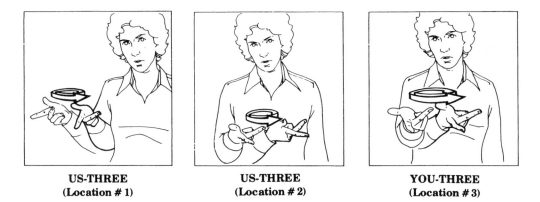

US-THREE	US-THREE	YOU-THREE
(Location # 1)	(Location # 2)	(Location # 3)

A similar process can be followed to refer to four or five people or things using the appropriate handshapes. (However, not all Signers will use this way of referring to five people or things). To refer to more than five, many Signers will either point with the index finger to each referent separately ('you and you and you . . .') or use a sweeping movement in an arc ('all of you' or 'all of them'). The honorific pronoun (see Unit 3) is also sometimes used with this arc in formal settings to refer to members of a group.

By now it should be clear that if the Signer is looking at person A and indexes (points to) person B, the meaning is 'him/her'. However, if the Signer is looking at B and indexes B, the meaning is 'you'. This shows how the direction of a Signer's eye gaze can change the meaning of some pronouns in ASL. However, it is also possible for Signers to use only eye gaze toward someone or something as a way of referring to that person or thing. Generally, this eye gaze is accompanied by a slight brow raise and a head nod or tilt toward the person or thing. In such cases there may be no manual signal (e.g. index) used.

If, for example, the Signer is talking with and looking at someone at a playground and signs

$$\overline{\text{WANT} \quad \text{PLAY}}^{\text{q}}$$

then the meaning is *You* wanna play?'. However, suppose the Signer is talking with someone at a playground where several other people are standing around, and a particular boy is standing to the Signer's right. If the Signer says

(gaze and nod to rt)
$$\text{WANT} \quad \text{PLAY,} \quad \overline{\text{\#OK}}^{\text{q}}$$

then the meaning is *He* wants to play. Is that alright with you?'. In this example, the eye gaze and head nod to the right acted as a way to reference the boy. These two examples show how a Signer can also use eye gaze and head movement as a 'pronoun'.

There are several related signs in ASL which can be used to indicate what is called "demonstrative reference". These signs convey the meaning 'that thing' or 'that one'. Illustrated below, these signs are used to refer to a specific (i.e. definite) person, place, or thing which is either present in the Signer's immediate environment or which has been assigned a specific location in space.

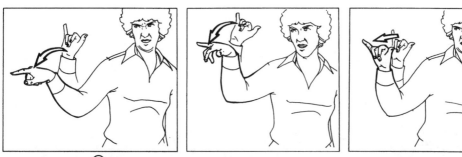

THAT-ONE‿INDEX-*rt*   THAT-ONE-*rt*   THAT-ONE*-*rt*

As discussed in Unit 3, Signers often use a kind of "reality principle" when assigning locations to people or things—the locations will reflect the actual (present or past) arrangement of the people or things. However, if the Signer doesn't know their actual locations, then obviously this "reality principle" cannot be used.

An alternate strategy involves assigning locations to people or things as they appear in the conversation or narrative, using a kind of "alternating pattern" of assignment. For example, many right-handed Signers will set up the first-mentioned person, place, or thing on their right; if there is a second person, place, or thing, it will be set up on their left. (Ref. = referent; i.e. the person, place, or thing)

Fig. 12.2

If there are three or more persons, places, or things which are to be assigned locations, then there are several possible ways to handle this, depending on the relationship between the people, places, or things. For example, if there are three people in a narrative, the Signer might use the locations shown in Figure 12.3. However, if two of the people form a pair or have a special relationship in contrast to the third person, then the Signer might use the locations shown in Figure 12.4.

Fig. 12.3   **Fig. 12.4**

Obviously, there is a limit to how many distinct locations can be established by the Signer (and remembered or perceived by the other person(s) in the conversation).

However, up to six separate locations can be comfortably assigned. For example, in describing a possible seating arrangement at a meeting, the Signer might use the six locations shown in Figure 12.5. Or, if the Signer is describing a panel discussion between two teams of three people, these same six locations might be used, but assigned in a slightly different order, as shown in Figure 12.6.

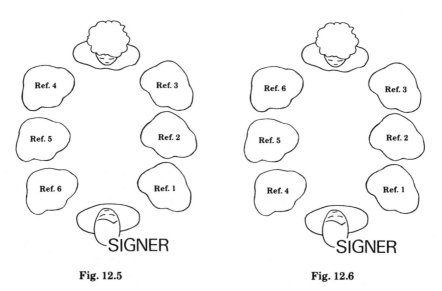

Fig. 12.5   Fig. 12.6

These are some of the strategies which Signers use for assigning referents to particular locations. Others will be discussed in later units.

G. Text Analysis

Pat₁: $\overline{\text{ONE-DAY-FUTURE NIGHT}\quad\overset{t}{\text{MOVIE,}}\quad\overset{q}{\text{YOU}\quad\text{GO-TO-}rt}}$

- **ONE-DAY-FUTURE NIGHT**

    In this situation, the meaning of these two joined signs is actually 'tomorrow night'. However, in some contexts when these two signs are used together, the meaning is 'the next night' or 'the following night'.

- $\overline{\overset{q}{}}$ **YOU   GO-TO-**rt

    Notice that the non-manual behaviors used here make this a 'yes-no' question. See Units 1 and 10 for a description of these non-manual behaviors.

    The sign **GO-TO-**rt is an example of a verb which can indicate the subject and/or object by its direction of movement. In this case, 'movie' (the object) has not previously been assigned a specific location. However, by moving the verb to the right, Pat has now clearly established the location of the 'movie'. Thus, if Pat or Lee wanted to refer to the 'movie' later on without using the sign **MOVIE**, they would use the location to Pat's right. See Units 4 and 13 for further discussion of verbs of this type.

Lee₁: $\overline{\text{MOVIE}\quad\text{CAPTION}\quad\overset{q}{\text{QMwg}}}$

- **QMwg**

    See Units 1 or 10 for a discussion of this question sign and some of its possible meanings.

Pat₂: $\overline{\overset{neg}{\text{INTERPRET+}}}$, $\overline{\text{KNOW+}\quad\text{WOMAN}\quad\overset{\text{(gaze rt,pursed lips)}}{\text{SMALL-}rt\quad\text{BLACK}\quad\text{H-A-I-R}}\quad\overset{\text{(rapid nodding}}{\text{THAT-ONE INDEX}}}$

- $\overset{neg}{\underline{}}$ **INTERPRET+**

    Notice that Pat responds to Lee's 'yes-no' question with the non-manual behaviors used to indicate negation. See Unit 1 for a discussion of these behaviors.

- **KNOW+ WOMAN $\overset{\text{(gaze rt,pursed lips)}}{\text{SMALL-}rt}$ BLACK H-A-I-R**

    Notice that Pat has assigned 'the woman' a location to the right. This was done by first gazing to the right and then signing **SMALL** to the right.

The non-manual signal *'pursed lips'* is seen in the photos below. The meanings of this signal are 'very small', 'very thin', or 'very narrow'. It can also mean that something is 'smooth', or that something happens 'quickly' or 'easily'. Here the obvious meaning is that the woman is very small or petite.

'very thin wire'   'very thin wire'

'smooth floor'   'very fast'

(rapid nodding   )
- **THAT-ONE‿INDEX-*rt***

This is a demonstrative pronoun. Notice that it is made in or toward the same location that was assigned to the woman—to Pat's right.

$$\overline{\text{nodding}}$$ $$\overline{\qquad\qquad\qquad\text{q}}$$
Lee$_2$:   SAME-AS EVERY-MORNING #TV THAT-ONE⁀INDEX-*lf*

- **EVERY-MORNING**

     This is an example of a sign used to indicate regularity.
     For further discussion and additional examples, see Unit
     11.

$$\overline{\qquad\qquad\qquad\text{q}}$$
- **THAT-ONE⁀INDEX-*lf***

     This is the same demonstrative pronoun that Pat used
     previously. Notice that Lee makes the sign to the left—
     the same location Pat used to refer to the woman. (Remem-
     ber if Pat and Lee are facing each other, then Pat's right
     is Lee's left.).
     Notice also that Lee uses the non-manual behaviors for
     asking a 'yes-no' question. Lee wants to know if the woman
     Pat described and the woman Lee is thinking of is the
     same person.

$$\overline{\text{nodding}}\qquad\overline{\quad\text{(gaze rt)}\quad}\quad\overline{\text{wh-q}}$$
Pat$_3$:   RIGHT++, US-TWO GO-*rt* WHY⁀NOT

- **US-TWO**

     Here Pat uses one of the two handshapes illustrated in the
     General Discussion section and moves it back and forth
     between him/herself and Lee.

- **GO-*rt***

     Notice that Pat again uses the location on the right to
     refer to the movie. Because this location refers to the
     movie, this sign could have been glossed as **GO**-*movie*.

- **WHY⁀NOT**

     Notice that the signs **WHY** and **NOT** are made in such a
     way that they look like one sign. Generally when this
     happens, there is some change in one of the two signs
     which helps the two signs look more like a single sign. In
     this case, the sign **WHY** is made close to the chin (the
     same location as the sign **NOT**), and there is a change in
     the handshape of the sign **WHY**.

neg						(gaze lf & rt⟵⟶)t		neg

Lee₃: **ME** (2h)**STAY**-*here,* **MOVIE** **INTERPRET** *me*-**LOOK-AT**-*lf & rt*⟵⟶, **NOT-LIKE*** **ME**

- **STAY**-*here*

  This is an example of a verb which indicates a specific place by the location in which it is produced (or toward which it is produced). See Units 4 and 13 for further discussion.

                    (gaze lf & rt⟵⟶   )t
- **MOVIE**   **INTERPRET**   *me*-**LOOK-AT**-*lf & rt*⟵⟶,

  Notice that the non-manual signal for a topic (see Unit 1) accompanies this portion of Lee's turn. Notice also that Lee's eye gaze matches or 'agrees with' the back and forth movement of the sign *me*-**LOOK-AT**-*lf & rt*⟵⟶.

  This is another example of a verb which can indicate the subject and/or object by means of its direction of movement. In this case, the meaning is something like 'looking back and forth between the movie and the interpreter'. See Units 4 and 13 for further discussion.

                    neg
- **NOT-LIKE***   **ME**

  The sign **NOT-LIKE*** is an example of what has been called *negative incorporation;* that is, the sign **LIKE** is negated by adding an outward, twisting movement (in addition to the *'neg'* signal behaviors). Only a small number of signs can be negated in this way—**KNOW, WANT, LIKE, GOOD.**

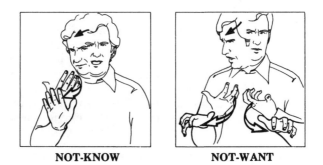

NOT-KNOW   NOT-WANT

Notice also that the sign **NOT-LIKE** is stressed and that negative non-manual behaviors occur throughout this portion of Lee's turn.

Pat₄: **THINK⁀YOURSELF,** ⟁ᵢ ,⟁ₐ ,   **US-THREE,**   t nod **GO-***rt*

- ⟁ᵢ , ⟁ₐ

  The signs ⟁ and ⟁ are name signs. According to one study of name signs, of 280 persons in the study, 42% were given their name signs at the age of 5 or before; 25% between the ages of 6 and 10; 15% between the ages of 11 and 15; and 18% at 16 years or older.

  One question that is often asked is "Where do people get their name signs?". According to this study of name signs, of 371 deaf persons asked, name signs were given by the following groups:

parents or family member	30%
residential school staff	13%
school peers	43%
work associates	10%
other	4%

  Thus, according to this information, most deaf people generally have a name sign before they are 10 years old, and it is generally given to them by their family or school peers.

- **US-THREE**

  The sign **US-THREE** is an example of a pronoun used to refer to three people. See the *General Discussion* section for more information.

Lee₅: ('happily surprised')
S-T-A-R-W-A-R-S-,   **ME**   *me*-**JOIN**-*you**   **GO-***lf**

- ('happily surprised')
  S-T-A-R-W-A-R-S,

  Notice that Lee fingerspells the name of the movie, repeating the last segment of Pat's turn. This type of feedback is often used as a way of checking with the Signer to see if his/her message was correctly understood. In this case, however, because of the non-manual behaviors it is obvious that Lee's repetition is due to surprise and delight at the name of the movie—not checking to see if s/he understood Pat's message.

- **GO-***lf**

  Notice that Lee is consistent in referring to the same location given to the movie by Pat. Notice also that this sign (and the sign *me*-**JOIN**-*you**) is stressed. Thus Lee indicates that s/he definitely wants to go to the movie.

H. Sample Drills

1. ONE-DAY-FUTURE NIGHT MOVIE,

_____t_____   _____q_____

MOVIE, YOU   GO-TO-*rt*
        |
        YOU-TWO
        |
        YOU-THREE
        |
        THOSE-TWO
        |
        THOSE-THREE
        |
        YOU-FOUR
        |
        US-TWO
        |
        US-THREE
        |
        US-FOUR
        |
        YOU

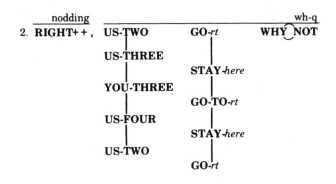

2. **RIGHT++** ,

nodding   _____wh-q_____

US-TWO   GO-*rt*   WHY NOT
| |
US-THREE |
| STAY-*here*
YOU-THREE |
| GO-TO-*rt*
US-FOUR |
| STAY-*here*
US-TWO |
              GO-*rt*

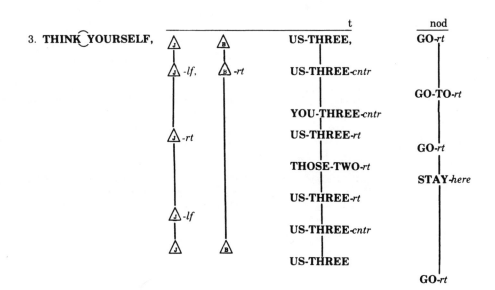

3. **THINK YOURSELF,**

_____t_____   ___nod___

                              US-THREE,   GO-*rt*
                              | |
                              US-THREE-*cntr* |
                                               GO-TO-*rt*
                              | |
                              YOU-THREE-*cntr* |
                              US-THREE-*rt* |
                                               GO-*rt*
                              THOSE-TWO-*rt* |
                                               STAY-*here*
                              US-THREE-*rt* |
                              US-THREE-*cntr* |
                              US-THREE |
                                               GO-*rt*

I. Video Notes

If you have access to the videotape package designed to accompany these texts, you will notice the following:

- Lee's final turn overlaps with Pat's final turn. Pat starts to fingerspell the title of the movie. However, as soon as Lee recognizes the title, she fingerspells it also. This type of copying or imitating behavior often occurs when a Signer fingerspells an unfamiliar word and the other person wants to make sure s/he has understood it correctly. In this case, however, the quick imitation shows Lee's recognition of the movie and surprise.

- Several examples of two signs being made together such that they look like a single sign. Notice the way the two signs flow together in **ONE-DAY-FUTURE NIGHT** (Pat$_2$), **THAT-ONE INDEX** (Pat$_2$, Lee$_2$), **WHY NOT** (Pat$_3$), and **THINK YOURSELF** (Pat$_4$).

- The name signs △ and △ are made on the back of the left wrist, and over the heart, respectively. Notice also that the sign **US-THREE** (Pat$_4$) is made close to the Signer in a location which clearly refers to the Signer, △ , and △ .

Unit 13

Subjects and Objects

A. Synopsis

Pat and Lee are having dinner at a restaurant. They have been talking about various schools for deaf students. Pat asks if Lee went to an oral school. Lee says that s/he went to one in New York. Pat asks what they do in oral schools. Lee says it's awful. Signs are forbidden and the teachers forced Lee to talk all the time. They'd get mad if s/he refused. Pat asks how Lee could understand if the teachers couldn't sign. Lee says it was hard; s/he had to read lips really carefully and make guesses. If s/he was wrong, the other children would tease and laugh at him/her. It was hard. Pat asks what would happen if s/he was wrong—would the teachers help Lee? Lee replies that sometimes they would bawl him/her out, and sometimes they would criticize him/her. And they would always tell Lee s/he had to practice and study hard. Pat says that reading lips and oralism is no good—signing is better. Lee agrees and says that every day when school was over and the children were out of the building, they would use ASL.

B. Cultural Information: Oral Schools and Programs

Oralism can be defined as an approach to communicating with deaf individuals (students or adults) through the use of speech, speechreading (lipreading), and hearing aids. People who advocate such an approach are often called *oralists*. Schools and programs which support this approach and use it as the primary means of communicating with deaf students are referred to as oral schools or oral programs. In most oral programs, the use of Sign Language or signing of any type is generally forbidden, and graduates of such programs report that they were often punished if teachers caught them signing or gesturing.

In the past (and even now), discussions about how to teach deaf students have quite often focused on the "oral-manual controversy"—with one group supporting the use of oral methods of education and the other supporting the use of some form of manual communication. During the eighteenth century, the major points of this controversy were expressed in an exchange of letters between Samuel Heinicke (founder of an oral school in Leipzig, Germany) and the Abbé Charles Michel de l'Epée (founder of a school which used signs in Paris, France). Interestingly enough, when Thomas Gallaudet went abroad in 1815 to learn about methods for educating deaf students, he went to oral schools in Great Britain (the Braidwood Schools) before he went to Epée's school in Paris.

The first oral school for deaf students in the United States—the Clarke School—was opened in Massachusetts in 1867. By the 1880's, there were eleven strictly oral schools in America. This growth was due, in large part, to the work and efforts of Alexander Graham Bell—who was an avowed oralist. Bell, whose wife was deaf, not only opposed the use of Sign Language but he also opposed intermarriage among deaf people. Bell donated a substantial portion of his fortune to oral schools and programs.

In 1890, an organization was established for teachers of deaf students and others who support oral methods of teaching deaf children. This organization, the Alexander Graham Bell Association for the Deaf (AGB), has as one of its main goals to aid schools in their efforts to teach speech, speechreading, and the use of residual hearing. The *Volta Review* is a regular publication of the AGB. For more information, contact: The Alexander Graham Bell Association for the Deaf, Inc., The Volta Bureau, 1537 35th Street, N.W., Washington, D.C. 20007.

C. Dialogue

Pat

Pat₁:
$$\overline{\hspace{7cm}}^{\text{q}}$$
YOU AWHILE-AGO SCHOOL ORAL RIGHT YOU

Pat₂:
$$\overline{\hspace{5cm}}^{\text{wh-q}}$$
#DO-DO ORAL SCHOOL #DO-DO

Pat₃:
$$\overline{\hspace{2cm}}^{(\text{'smile'})\text{q}}\quad\overline{\hspace{5cm}}^{\text{wh-q}}$$
TEACH⌒AGENT SIGN INEPT,   RIGHT, HOWwg UNDERSTAND HOWwg

Pat₄:
$$\overline{\hspace{2cm}}^{\text{cond}}\quad\overline{\hspace{5cm}}^{\text{q}}$$
SUPPOSE WRONG, TEACH⌒AGENT *teachers*-HELP-*you*

Pat₅:
$$\overline{\hspace{3cm}}^{\text{t}}$$
ORAL, READ-*lips*, (2h)#NG, BETTER SIGN BETTER

Pat₆: (2h)"WELL" (signed with Lee's "WELL")

Lee

Lee₁:
<u>nodding</u>   (gaze rt)
        RIGHT, INDEX-*rt* NEW-YORK, RIGHT YOU

Lee₂:
               <u>t</u>
"PSHAW" AWFUL, SIGN, NOT-LEGAL,

<u>   t   </u>
TEACH⁀AGENT INDEX-*arc-rt*, *teachers*-FORCE-*me* ME SPEAK"*over & over again*",

<u>   cond </u>   <u>   pow </u>
SUPPOSE ME REFUSE ME *me*-SAY-#NO-TO-*teachers*, (2h)BECOME-ANGRY INDEX-*arc-rt*

Lee₃:
        <u>nodding</u>
"WELL" HARD+, ME READ-*lips*,

        (gaze up,rt; 'struggling to understand'   )
ME *me*-LOOK-AT-*teachers*"*over time*" READ-*lips* (2h)alt.GUESS,

<u>   cond </u>(gaze lf   )   <u>t</u>
SUPPOSE ME WRONG, CHILDREN-*lf* INDEX-*arc-lf*,

children-MAKE-FUN-OF-*me* *children*-TEASE-*me*, "WELL" HARD (2h)"PSHAW"

Lee₄:
              <u>t</u>   <u>puff.cheeks</u>
"WELL", SOMETIMES, *teachers*-BAWL-OUT-*me*"*regularly*",

         <u>t</u>   <u>puff.cheeks</u>
SOMETIMES, *teachers*-CRITICIZE-*me*"*regularly*",

EVERY-DAY TEACH⁀AGENT *teachers*-TELL-*me*"*over & over again*"

      (gaze up,rt   ) (gaze up,rt   )
MUST PRACTICE"*over & over again*" STUDY"*over & over again*"

Lee₅:
<u>nodding</u>
        ME *me*-AGREE-WITH-*you* ME,

                <u>(gaze lf & rt   )</u>   <u>rhet.q</u>   <u>puff.cheeks</u>
EVERY-DAY CHILDREN SCHOOL FINISH, OUT-OF-*school*,   USE-ASL "WELL"

D. Key Illustrations

Pat

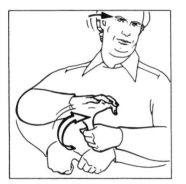

ORAL

RIGHT

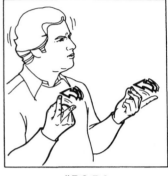

#DO-DO

INEPT

HOWwg

teachers-HELP-*you*

(2h)#NG

Lee

NOT-LEGAL

teachers-**FORCE**-*me*

SPEAK *"over & over again"*

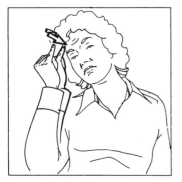

SUPPOSE

me-**SAY**-**#** **NO-TO**-*teachers*

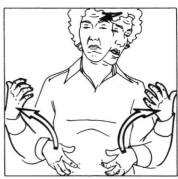

BECOME-ANGRY

READ-*lips*

me-**LOOK-AT**-*teachers* *"over time"*

(2h)alt.GUESS

children-MAKE-FUN-OF-*me*

children-TEASE-*me*

teachers-BAWL-OUT-*me"regularly"*

teachers-CRITICIZE-*me"regularly"*

me-AGREE-WITH-*you*

E. Supplementary Illustrations

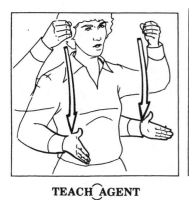

TEACH⌣AGENT

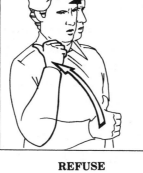

REFUSE

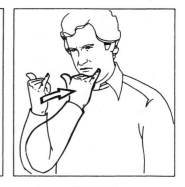

WRONG

EVERY-DAY

F. General Discussion: Subjects and Objects

Before reading this section, it will be helpful to review the discussion of subjects and objects in Unit 4. That unit described how certain verbs in ASL can make use of the space around the Signer's body (or locations on the Signer's body) to indicate the subject and/or object. This discussion will expand on some of the information in Unit 4 as well as introduce the reader to reciprocal verbs and direct address.

As illustrated in Unit 4, many verbs in ASL use the assigned spatial locations of persons, places, or things to show who is doing something (the subject) or who is receiving that action (the direct or indirect object) or where the action occurs (the oblique object). This is accomplished by moving the sign from one location to another, or by making the sign in a particular location. Thus, the meaning 'I give him/her' is expressed by moving the verb ____-GIVE-TO-____ from the Signer toward the 'third person'; the meaning 's/he gives me' is expressed by moving the verb from the 'third person' toward the Signer.

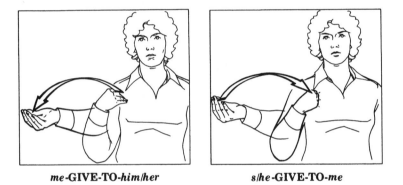

me-**GIVE-TO**-*him/her*   *s/he*-**GIVE-TO**-*me*

With some other verbs that are made with both hands, the location of the non-dominant hand is also important. For example, the signs *you*-**FLATTER**-*me* and *s/he*-**FLATTER**-*me* share the same basic movement and palm orientation, but their locations are different.

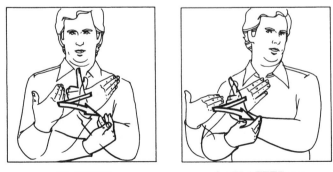

you-**FLATTER**-*me*   *s/he*-**FLATTER**-*me*

The following is a partial list of the *directional verbs* in ASL which appear in the student texts.

____-ARREST-____	____-LOOK-AT-____
____-ASK-TO-____	____-MAKE-CONTACT-WITH-____
____-BAWL-OUT-____	____-MAKE-FUN-OF-____
____-BLAME-____	____-MOOCH-FROM-____
____-BORROW-FROM-____	____-PARTICIPATE/JOIN-____
____-BOTHER-____	____-PAY-TO-____
____-COLLIDE-WITH-____	____-PITY-____
____-CRITICIZE-____	____-QUIT-____
____-GIVE-TO-____	____-SAY-#NO-TO-____
____-HATE-____	____-SAY-#OK-TO-____
____-HELP-____	____-SAY-#YES-TO-____
____-INFLUENCE-____	____-SEND-TO-____
____-INFORM-____	____-TEACH-____
____-INSULT-____	____-TTY-CALL-TO-____
____-JOIN-TO-____	

Some directional verbs are *reciprocal;* that is, by using both hands, a Signer can indicate that two people or two groups do the same thing to each other. In a sense, each hand represents the action of one person or group. Again, the location of the hands, their direction of movement, and/or their palm orientation show which persons or groups are involved in the action. For example, notice how the meanings 'they look at each other' and 'we look at each other' are expressed in the illustrations below. The sign on the left indicates that there are two 'third persons' (one on the right and one on the left) which do the same thing to each other. The sign on the right indicates that the Signer and 'second person' do the same thing to each other.

they-LOOK-AT-"each other"   *we*-LOOK-AT-*"each other"*

Verbs normally made with two hands also become reciprocal by moving the hands from the two separate locations toward each other. For example, the sign ____-**INFORM**-____ is usually made with both hands. To express a reciprocal action (e.g. 'they inform each other', 'we inform each other'), each hand moves from one of the locations toward the other location.

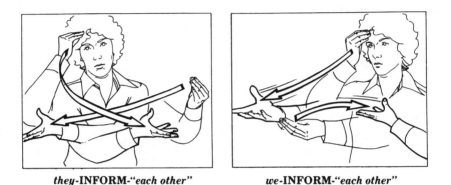

they-**INFORM**-*"each other"*   *we*-**INFORM**-*"each other"*

Some verbs are always reciprocal because of their meanings—for example, ____-**CHANGE-PLACE-WITH**-____ and ____-**QUARREL-WITH**-____. Again, with these verbs the Signer will clearly indicate which two people or groups are changing places or quarreling with each other.

Unit 4 also described how certain verbs can indicate an action or state of being at a particular location on the body. This is done by making the sign at or on that specific location. For example, the signs **SHAVE**-____ and **HAVE-OPERATION-ON**-____ can be made in various locations on the Signer's body to indicate where that action occurs.

 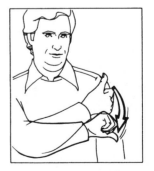

SHAVE-*face*   **HAVE-OPERATION-ON**-*upper arm*

The following is a partial list of verbs that can use specific body locations to indicate where an action occurs.

BANG-ON-_____

BITE-(ON)-_____

BLEED-FROM-_____

HAVE-FRECKLES-ON-_____

HAVE-OPERATION-ON-_____

HAVE-PAIN-AT-_____

HAVE-RASH-ON-_____

HIT-(ON)-_____

#HURT-(AT)-_____

KISS-(ON)-_____

PERSPIRE-FROM-_____

PUSH-(ON)-_____

SCRATCH-(AT)-_____

SHAVE-(AT)-_____

TAP-ON-_____

WASH-(AT)-_____

Another commonly used strategy for indicating 'who' does something is body shifting and eye gaze shifting. For example, the Signer may move his/her body to the left or to the right 'into' a location that represents someone. While 'in' that location, everything the Signer says or does reflects what that person says or does. When this kind of body shifting into a location (and looking *from* that location) is used, the Signer also tends to copy certain characteristic facial expressions or other behaviors of the person s/he has 'become'.

For example, suppose the Signer is describing an incident that occurred while she was in elementary school. During this incident, a younger and smaller student came up to the Signer and asked if the Signer wanted to fight. By body shifting into a location slightly to the left and by gazing to the right and upward, the Signer can 'become' the smaller student who then asks for a fight. By shifting back and gazing to the left and downward, the Signer can 'become' herself again and respond "You're not worth it".

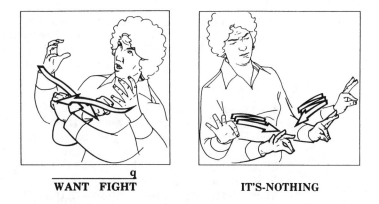

_____q
WANT FIGHT   IT'S-NOTHING

Body and gaze shifting like this has the effect of putting what is said 'in quotes', indicating *what* was said and *who* said it. When the Signer wants to discontinue this direct quoting behavior and add his/her own comments, then the body will shift to its normal position and the Signer will again look at the person s/he is talking with. This type of direct quoting (called *direct address*) occurs quite frequently in ASL.

This discussion has reviewed how some directional verbs indicate their subject and/or object. It has also described how certain verbs can become reciprocal. Finally, it has described how Signers use body and gaze shifting to indicate direct address. Future units will provide additional examples and discussion of these important features of ASL.

G. Text Analysis

$$\overline{}^{\,t}$$

Lee₂: "PSHAW" AWFUL, $\overline{\text{SIGN,}}$ NOT-LEGAL,

$$\overline{}^{\,t}$$

TEACH‿AGENT INDEX-*arc-rt*, *teachers*-**FORCE**-*me*   **ME** **SPEAK**″*over & over again*″,

$$\overline{}^{\,cond}$$

SUPPOSE **ME** **REFUSE** **ME** *me*-**SAY-#NO-TO**-*teachers*, (2h)**BECOME-ANGRY** **INDEX**-*arc-rt*

$$\overline{}^{\,t}$$

- **TEACH‿AGENT**   **INDEX**-*arc-rt*,

  Notice that the sign **TEACH‿AGENT** is another example of two signs which can be produced in such a way that they look like a single sign. However, with verbs like **TEACH** and **PREACH**, Signers do not always use the **AGENT** sign to form the nouns 'teacher' or 'preacher'. Instead, these nouns can alternately be formed by using short tense movements (usually two), without the sign **AGENT**.

  The sign **INDEX**-*arc-rt* is a plural pronoun which indicates that the referent of **TEACH‿AGENT** is plural and assigns a location (Lee's right) to the 'teachers'. For further discussion of plural pronouns, see Units 3 and 12.

- *teachers*-**FORCE**-*me*

  This is an example of a verb which can indicate its subject (teachers) and its object (me) by the direction of its movement. Since 'teachers' has been established to the Signer's right, the verb moves from the right toward the Signer.

- **SPEAK**″*over & over again*″

  This is an example of one of the verb modulations used in ASL to indicate temporal aspect. (See Units 8 and 17 for further information.) This particular modulation is made with a somewhat tense straight-line 'thrust' followed by an arc-like movement back to the starting point and a forward rocking motion of the body and/or head with each 'thrust'. This movement is shown in the following illustration:

  cond

- **SUPPOSE ME REFUSE ME** *me*-**SAY-#NO-TO**-*teachers,*

> This is the *condition* part (If . . .) of a conditional sentence. See Unit 10 for a description of the non-manual behaviors which are used to indicate conditionals. Notice that the sign *me*-**SAY-#NO-TO**-*teachers* is a fingerspelled loan sign which can indicate its subject and/or object by means of the direction of its movement. Two other fingerspelled loan signs that can function in this way are ____-**SAY-#OK-TO**-____ and ____-**SAY-#YES-TO**-____.

                                          ('smile')q   wh-q

Pat₃: **TEACH͡ AGENT SIGN ĨNEPT,**   **RIGHT,** **HOWwg UNDERSTAND HOWwg**

                 ('smile')q

- **RIGHT,**

> Notice that Pat makes a statement and then asks Lee if it is correct or not. Since Lee responds by nodding, Pat continues with his/her turn and asks Lee another question.

                     nodding

Lee₃: **"WELL" HARD+,** **ME** **READ**-*lips,*

           (gaze up,rt; 'struggling to understand'   )
   ME *me*-**LOOK-AT**-*teachers"over time"* **READ**-*lips* **(2h)alt.GUESS,**

                              cond   (gaze lf   )   t
  SUPPOSE **ME** **WRONG,** **CHILDREN**-*lf* **INDEX**-*arc-lf,*

  children-**MAKE-FUN-OF**-*me* *children*-**TEASE**-*me,* **"WELL"** **HARD** **(2h)"PSHAW"**

- *me*-**LOOK-AT**-*teachers"over time"*

> This is an example of a verb which can indicate the subject and object by its direction of movement. (See *General Discussion* section above and Chapter 4 for more information.)
>
> In this context (following the verb **READ**-*lips)*, the sign indicates that Lee was trying to read the teacher's lips.
>
> Notice also that this verb is produced with the modulation written as *"over time"*. This particular modulation is made with a repeated, small circular motion.

Units 8 and 17 provide further information about verb modulations which indicate temporal aspect.

- **READ**-*lips*

    This verb indicates the object 'lips' by being produced at that location of the Signer's body. Similarly, it could mean 'read mind' if produced at the forehead. Notice that this verb could be glossed as **LOOK-AT**-*lips"over time"*, but has the specific meaning of 'reading lips'.

                                cond

- **SUPPOSE   ME   WRONG,**

    This is another example of a *condition* in a conditional sentence. See Unit 10 for a description of the non-manual behaviors used for conditionals.

  (gaze lf   )   t

- **CHILDREN**-*lf*   **INDEX**-*arc-lf,*

    Although the sign **CHILDREN** has been signed to the left, the Signer also uses the pronoun **INDEX**-*arc-lf* to clearly locate the children to the left and, thus, clearly separate the children and the teachers. Notice that the **INDEX** is made plural *(arc)* to 'agree with' the plural noun— **CHILDREN.**

- *children*-**MAKE-FUN-OF**-*me*   *children*-**TEASE**-*me*

    Because the Signer has clearly established the children to the left and because the direction of movement of these two signs is from the left, it is clear that the children (and not the teachers) made fun of and teased the Signer.
    Notice that the sign ____-**MAKE-FUN-OF**-____ can easily be made reciprocal, but the sign ____-**TEASE**-____ is more constrained because of the way it is made.

                    cond   q

Pat$_4$:   **SUPPOSE   WRONG,   TEACH͡AGENT**   *teachers*-**HELP**-*you*

    This is another example of a conditional sentence. Remember that in ASL the condition is generally stated first, followed by the result or consequence. Notice here that the result is a question. That is, the Signer asks a question about the result.

- *teachers*-**HELP**-*you*

    Notice that with this directional verb, Pat uses the location assigned by Lee to the 'teachers' (i.e. Lee's right and Pat's left). Thus, the sign moves from Pat's left toward Lee.

<pre>
                         _____t   _____puff.cheeks
Lee₄: "WELL", SOMETIMES,   teachers-BAWL-OUT-me"regularly",
</pre>

<pre>
              _____t   _____puff.cheeks
         SOMETIMES,   teachers-CRITICIZE-me"regularly",
</pre>

EVERY-DAY TEACH⁀AGENT   *teachers-TELL-me"over & over again"*

<pre>
              (gaze up,rt   ) (gaze up,rt   )
    MUST   PRACTICE"over & over again"   STUDY"over & over again"
</pre>

<pre>
                                 _____puff.cheeks
</pre>
- *teachers-**BAWL-OUT**-me"regularly"*,

  The sign ____-**BAWL-OUT**-____ is a directional verb. That is, the direction of movement indicates who is the subject and who is the object. Notice that the sign occurs with the verb modulation *"regularly"*. (This is described in Unit 8). The meaning that this special movement conveys is that the action ('bawling me out') happens 'frequently, a lot, or regularly'. This is also supported by the *'puff.cheeks'* signal which conveys the meaning 'a lot; huge number of; of great magnitude'.

<pre>
                                 _____puff.cheeks
</pre>
- *teachers-**CRITICIZE**-me"regularly"*

  This verb is like the verb ____-**BAWL-OUT**-____ discussed above. It is a directional verb with the verb modulation that indicates the action occurred 'frequently, a lot, or regularly'. It is also accompanied by the *'puff.cheeks'* signal.

- *teachers-**TELL**-me"over & over again"*

  This is also a verb which can indicate its subject and object by the direction of its movement. Notice that this verb has the same modulation as the verb **SPEAK** in Lee's second turn and the following verb **STUDY**. This particular modulation indicates that the action occurred again and again for a long time.

<pre>
         ___nodding
Lee₅: ME   me-AGREE-WITH-you   ME,
</pre>

<pre>
                      (gaze lf & rt   )   rhet.q   puff.cheeks
         EVERY-DAY CHILDREN SCHOOL FINISH, OUT-OF-school,   USE-ASL "WELL"
</pre>

- *me-**AGREE-WITH**-you*

  This is an example of a verb which is normally made with both hands. With this form of the verb, *me-**AGREE-WITH**-you*, both hands generally move from the Signer toward the person s/he is talking with. The sign could be made reciprocal by moving one hand from the Signer toward the other person, while the other hand moves from that person toward the Signer. Notice how the hands move from the two people toward each other in the illustration below—which shows the Signer asking two people if they agree with each other.

_____q
you-AGREE-WITH-*"each other"*

<u>puff.cheeks</u>
- **USE-ASL**

    Notice that since the signal *'puff.cheeks'* means 'a lot' or 'of great magnitude', Lee is indicating that the children used ASL a lot.

H. Sample Drills

                             _____cond

1.   **SUPPOSE ME WRONG, CHILDREN**-*lf* **INDEX**-*arc-lf* *children*-**MAKE-FUN-OF**-*me*

                                                             children-**TEASE**-*me*

                                                             children-**CRITICIZE**-*me*

                                                             children-**TELL**-*me*

                                                             children-**BAWL-OUT**-*me*

                                                             children-**HELP**-*me*

                                                             children-**CRITICIZE**-*me*

                                                             children-**MAKE-FUN-OF**-*me*

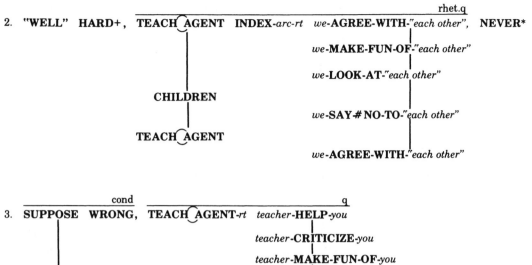

2. "WELL" HARD+, TEACH⌒AGENT INDEX-*arc-rt* *we*-**AGREE-WITH**-*"each other"*, **NEVER***

| rhet.q
| ————————
| *we*-**MAKE-FUN-OF**-*"each other"*

| *we*-**LOOK-AT**-*"each other"*

| **CHILDREN**

| *we*-**SAY#NO-TO**-*"each other"*

| **TEACH⌒AGENT**

| *we*-**AGREE-WITH**-*"each other"*

        cond   q
      ————————   ——————————————————————
3. **SUPPOSE WRONG**, **TEACH⌒AGENT**-*rt* *teacher*-**HELP**-*you*

| *teacher*-**CRITICIZE**-*you*

| *teacher*-**MAKE-FUN-OF**-*you*

| **#IF**   *teacher*-**TEASE**-*you*

| *teacher*-**BAWL-OUT**-*you*

| *teacher*-**HELP**-*you*

| *teacher*-**BAWL-OUT**-*you**

| **SUPPOSE**

| *teacher*-**HELP**-*you*

I. Video Notes

If you have access to the videotape package designed to accompany these texts, you will notice the following:

- The range of non-manual signals which occur in the dialogue to indicate topics (Lee$_2$, Lee$_3$, Lee$_4$, Pat$_5$), 'yes-no' questions (Pat$_1$, Pat$_3$, Pat$_4$), 'wh-word' questions (Pat$_2$, Pat$_3$), and conditionals (Lee$_3$, Pat$_4$). Also notice the *'puff.cheeks'* signals (Lee$_4$, Lee$_5$).

- In Pat's third turn, he asks a 'yes-no' question, but since Lee responds affirmatively by nodding her head, Pat continues his turn and asks a 'wh-word' question. Also, notice that Pat smiles while asking the 'yes-no' question. In this case, the smile seems to indicate that he already knows that the answer to the question will be 'yes'.

- Notice that Lee uses three of the verb modulations which indicate temporal aspect: *"over time"* (Lee$_3$), *"over & over again"* (Lee$_2$, Lee$_4$) and *"regularly"* (Lee$_4$).

- Notice that when Lee uses the verb modulation *"over & over again"* (Lee$_4$), she also uses a non-manual signal which adds the meanings 'too much' and 'hard'.

Unit 14

Classifiers

A. Synopsis

Pat and Lee are friends who meet on a street corner. Pat asks Lee why s/he didn't go to the Deaf club last night. Lee couldn't make it because his/her brother came over at 3 PM and the two of them talked for a long time. Pat asks what did Lee's brother want. Lee explains that next summer his/her brother wants to bring his family to stay with Lee. Lee is strongly opposed to that so the two of them ended up struggling with each other all night. Pat feels sorry for Lee and says that last night they painted and changed things around a lot at the club. Lee asks what they changed and what they did. Pat says that they took down all the old state school pictures and painted the wall white. Lee doesn't like white and says that green is better. Pat adds that they also took all the bowling trophies down, put them in a box and threw them out. Lee notes that the club has really improved a lot.

B. Cultural Information: Deaf Clubs

The National Association of the Deaf (NAD) currently has listings of well over 175 different Deaf Clubs in the United States. Many of these Clubs have been established to serve specific functions or to serve the needs of special sub-groups of the Deaf Community. Names such as the Maryland Senior Citizens Deaf Club, Fresno Athletic Club of the Deaf, Ebony Social Club of the Deaf, 47 Alumni Association, Utah Sportsmen Club of the Deaf, Angel West Catholic Club provide some indication as to the wide range of social, political, religious, and recreational functions which Deaf Clubs serve.

Historically, the Deaf Club fulfilled a vital need in the lives of members of the Deaf Community—it provided a place where members of the Community could meet to share their ideas, interests, and language. Before captioned films (Unit 11) became available and before the increasing national sensitivity toward Deaf people, the Deaf Club often provided the only form of social life for its members. In addition, Club members would often share valuable information with each other, like which of the doctors, lawyers, and dentists were sensitive and understanding, where certain services could be obtained from people who could be trusted, etc. In short, the Club often functioned as a place where Deaf people could seek and give advice on how to best deal with the hearing world.

At the present time, however, because of the increased availability of interpreters and the increased number of hearing people who are learning Sign, this function of the Deaf Club seems to be declining. In addition, because a wider range of social activities are now accessible to Deaf people, the Deaf Club is no longer the only social outlet for many Deaf people. Consequently, the role and function of the Deaf Club in the lives of many Deaf people is changing.

Most Clubs are open at specific times. However, these times range from, for example, "every Thursday, Friday and Saturday evening" to "every third Friday of the month". Very often Clubs arrange for captioned films, social evenings, athletic events, etc., for their members. Many Clubs sponsor basketball and softball teams which compete with each other under the auspices of the American Athletic Association of the Deaf, Inc. (AAAD). In addition, many Deaf Clubs publish monthly newsletters to keep their members informed of local and national events.

C. Dialogue

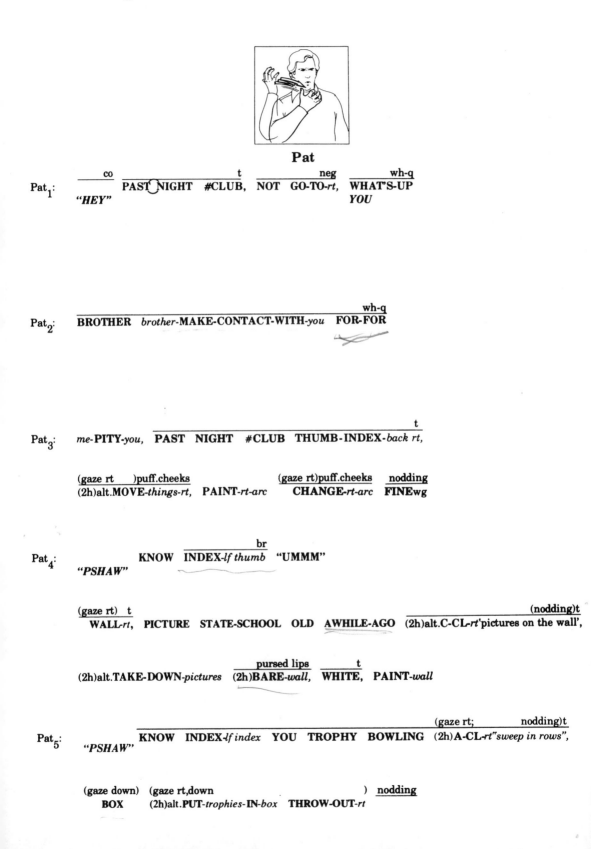

Pat

          co   t   neg   wh-q
Pat₁: _____ _____ _____
       PAST NIGHT #CLUB, NOT GO-TO-*rt*, WHAT'S-UP
       "HEY"   *YOU*

                                                               wh-q
       _____ _____
Pat₂: **BROTHER** *brother*-MAKE-CONTACT-WITH-*you* **FOR-FOR**

                                                                    t
       _____ __
Pat₃: *me*-**PITY**-*you*, **PAST NIGHT #CLUB THUMB-INDEX**-*back rt*,

       (gaze rt   )puff.cheeks   (gaze rt)puff.cheeks   nodding
       _____   _____   _____
       (2h)alt.MOVE-*things-rt*, **PAINT**-*rt-arc*   **CHANGE**-*rt-arc*   **FINE**wg

                                      br
                            _____
Pat₄: **KNOW INDEX**-*lf thumb* **"UMMM"**
       "PSHAW"

       (gaze rt) t   (nodding)t
       _____ _____   _____
       WALL-*rt*, **PICTURE STATE-SCHOOL OLD AWHILE-AGO** **(2h)alt.C-CL**-*rt*'pictures on the wall',

                            pursed lips   t
                       _____   _____
       (2h)alt.TAKE-DOWN-*pictures* **(2h)BARE**-*wall*, **WHITE**, **PAINT**-*wall*

                                                         (gaze rt;   nodding)t
       _____   _____
Pat₅: **KNOW INDEX**-*lf index* **YOU TROPHY BOWLING** **(2h)A-CL**-*rt*"sweep in rows",
       "PSHAW"

       (gaze down) (gaze rt,down   ) nodding
       _____   _____   _____
          BOX   **(2h)alt.PUT**-*trophies*-**IN**-*box* **THROW-OUT**-*rt*

Lee

Lee₁:
                                         t   (gaze rt   )
  (2h)"WELL" STUCK ME, ONE-DAY-PAST TIME⌢THREE, BROTHER *brother(rt)*-MEET-*me*

    (gaze rt)   nod   (gaze rt)
    V:-CL@*rt,out* ⎱ 'sit facing each other', CHAT*"long time"*
    V:-CL@*rt,in* ⎰

Lee₂:
    (gaze rt)   *topic*   puff.cheeks
  INDEX-*rt* NEXT SUMMER, WANT F̲AMILY FROM-*rt*-GROUP-COME-TO-*here*,

                        neg
  ME NOT-WANT++, US-TWO-*rt* STRUGGLE*"regularly"* ALL-NIGHT

Lee₃:
                            wh-q
  "WHAT" CHANGE #DO-DO

Lee₄:
  WHITE YECCH-*rt*, BETTER GREEN BETTER

Lee₅:
                                    nodding
  #CLUB CHANGE, IMPROVE* TRUE "HMMM"

D. Key Illustrations

Pat

WHAT'S-UP

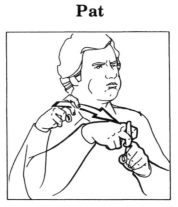

brother-**MAKE-CONTACT-WITH**-*you*

me-**PITY**-*you*

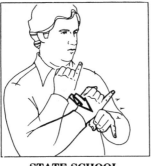

STATE-SCHOOL

(2h)alt.C-CL'pictures on wall'

(2h)alt.TAKE-DOWN-*pictures*

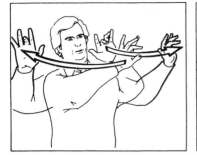

(2h)BARE-*wall*

PAINT-*wall*

(2h)alt.PUT-*trophies*-**IN**-*box*

Lee

TIME C THREE

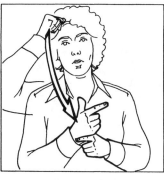

BROTHER

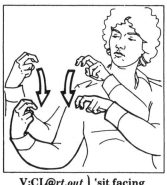

V:CL@*rt,out* ⎫ 'sit facing
V:CL@*rt,in* ⎬ each other'

CHAT *"long time"*

STRUGGLE *"regularly"*

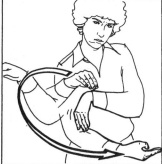

ALL-NIGHT

CHANGE

YECCH-*rt*

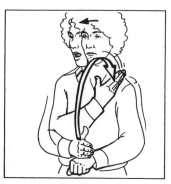

IMPROVE*

E. Supplementary Illustrations

PAST⌒NIGHT

FOR-FOR

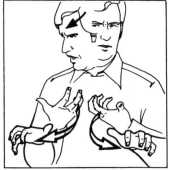

NOT-WANT

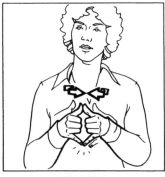

TROPHY

(2h)A-CL*"sweep in rows"*

F. General Discussion: Classifiers

Unit 5 briefly described some uses of classifiers, the need to clearly identify what each classifier represents, the way some SASSes provide information about the size, shape, or texture of things, and how classifiers are used in certain conventional signs. This discussion will provide more information on some of those topics but will focus on ways to show that something is plural with classifiers. The final section will describe how classifier handshapes are used in certain verbs.

As stated in Unit 5, many classifiers stand for or represent a particular group or "class" of nouns. Generally, this type of classifier is not used until the Signer has clearly identified which noun it stands for. In the sense that classifiers represent nouns, they function as pronouns. Many classifiers can also function as verbs because they can move. In addition, classifiers can convey information about the manner of an action (e.g. fast, slow, uneven). Finally, classifiers show where people or things are located in space and, thus, can show the locative relationships between those people or things.

If most of the classifiers in ASL are singular (i.e. they represent one thing), how can a Signer represent more than one thing? One obvious way is to use classifiers on both hands. This was seen in Unit 5 when the Signer (Pat) represented the actions of two cars by using both hands.

3→CL'car stopped'
3→CL'car smash into stopped car'

However, suppose the Signer cannot or chooses not to use both hands? Or, suppose the Signer wishes to represent more than two things? How can this be done? As described in Unit 7, one general strategy is to use some form of repetition. Each time the classifier is repeated, it is given a different location. This repetition can be done with one hand or with both hands (each having the appropriate classifier handshape).

When both hands are used in an alternating manner, it shows that there are several-to-many people or things located in many different places in an unorderly manner. For example, the A-CL can be used to represent a trophy, statue, bottle, can, etc. If the Signer wants to indicate that there are many statues all around a room, s/he may use this classifier with a two-handed, alternating movement.

(2h)alt.A-CL

When the Signer wants to indicate that the statues are arranged in an orderly fashion (e.g. in a row), then s/he will repeat the classifier in a straight line. (The non-dominant hand often 'holds' the starting place.) If the Signer wants to show that there is more than one row of these things, then the Signer simply repeats the classifier in more than one row.

(2h)A-CL*"in a row"*   (2h)A-CL*"in rows"*

Suppose that there are *many* things in a row. The Signer would probably use what is called a "sweep". Here, instead of moving the classifier in a clear and distinct manner, it moves (sweeps) straight across the row. Likewise, if the Signer wanted to indicate *many* things in more than one row, s/he would simply repeat this sweeping motion in more than one row.

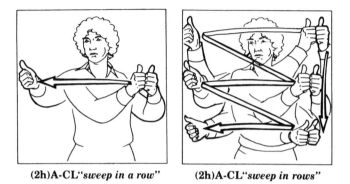

(2h)A-CL*"sweep in a row"*   (2h)A-CL*"sweep in rows"*

Thus, one way to show that there is more than one of something is to use some form of repetition with a singular classifier. This repetition will also provide information about the relative number of things (e.g. several, many) and the way they are arranged (e.g. in a disorderly manner, in rows).

Another way to indicate plurality is to use a plural classifier. There are two types of plural classifiers: classifiers which represent a specific number (e.g. three), and classifiers which represent 'many' things or people. Specific-number classifiers use the handshapes for numbers (e.g. 2, 3, 4, 5) and, like the **1-CL,** they represent a specific number of people. For example, the **2-CL** could represent two women who walk up to the Signer, as illustrated below.

2-CL'come up to me from rt'

When both hands (with either the '4' or '5' handshape) are used *together,* they no longer represent a specific number of individuals but represent a group of many individuals. For example, the (2h)4-CL could be used to represent a row of people who are standing. Or, by using the 4:-CL, the Signer can represent a group of people who are seated in semi-circle. The direction in which the palms face will indicate which direction the people are facing.

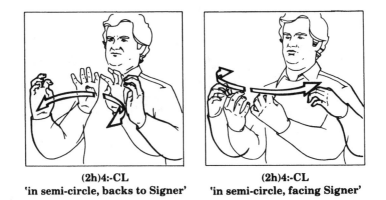

<table>
<tr><td align="center">(2h)4:-CL
'in semi-circle, backs to Signer'</td><td align="center">(2h)4:-CL
'in semi-circle, facing Signer'</td></tr>
</table>

There are several other plural classifiers which use the '4' or '5' handshapes but generally have the palm facing downward. These also represent groups and can be made with one or both hands, although the use of both hands generally indicates that the group is very large.

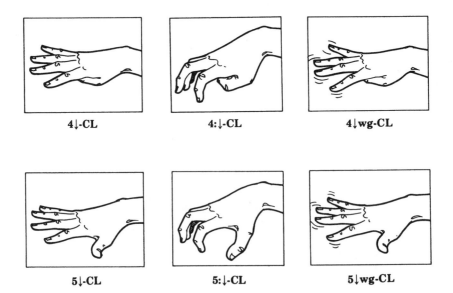

<table>
<tr><td align="center">4↓-CL</td><td align="center">4:↓-CL</td><td align="center">4↓wg-CL</td></tr>
<tr><td align="center">5↓-CL</td><td align="center">5:↓-CL</td><td align="center">5↓wg-CL</td></tr>
</table>

These classifiers can represent a wide variety of things (e.g. cats, rocks, stairs, chairs, shoes, insects), not just people. The choice of which classifier to use in a particular situation depends upon such factors as whether the group of things is moving or not, or whether the things are viewed as being arranged in a particular order or not.

For example, if the Signer signed **COW** and then the classifier (2h)**5:↓-CL,** the meaning would be 'there is a huge herd of cattle'. This classifier does not indicate if the cattle are stationary or moving; it could be used in either case and only indicates that there is a 'huge herd'. If the Signer wants to show that the cattle are moving, s/he would use either the **5↓wg-CL** or the **5↓-CL.** The one with 'wiggly' fingers suggests that the cattle are moving in an unorderly manner—like you would see if they stampeded away in a panic, or were just 'milling around'. The **5↓-CL** would indicate a more smooth, orderly movement with all of the cattle moving together in the same direction.

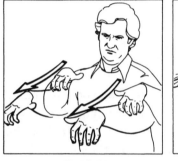 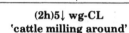 

(2h)5:↓-CL	(2h)5↓ wg-CL	(2h)5↓-CL
'huge herd of cattle'	**'cattle milling around'**	**'mass of cattle moving outward'**

Another classifier used to represent a group is made with both hands with 'C' handshapes—(2h)**C-CL**'group'. This classifier (frequently glossed as **CLASS** or **GROUP**) is often used to assign spatial locations to groups of people or things. It can also be moved in space as a verb. By bringing the hands and fingers closer together or farther apart, the Signer can indicate the relative size of the group.

 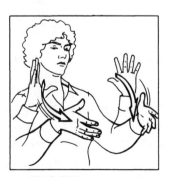

(2h)C-CL'small group'	(2h)C-CL'large group'

Classifier handshapes can also be used in certain verbs. For example, **PICK-UP-____**, **TAKE-____**, and **POUR-FROM-____** are verbs in which the handshape often changes to fit certain physical characteristics of the thing that is picked up, taken, poured from, etc. For example, as described in Unit 5, the **F-CL** can refer to a coin, button, marble, etc. If the Signer is talking about 'picking up a coin', then s/he may use that 'F' handshape in the verb (or a variant—the 'open F' handshape in which the thumb and index finger do not contact).

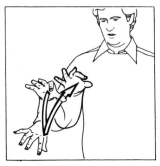

PICK-UP-*coin*

Notice that the choice of handshape depends on the size or shape or some other physical characteristic of the object. Thus, verbs which alter their handshape in this way provide information about which thing is the object. For example, to describe the act of picking up a 'marble', a 'cup', and a 'rock' one-by-one, the Signer would use different handshapes, as illustrated below.

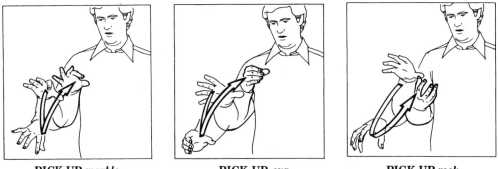

PICK-UP-*marble*   PICK-UP-*cup*   PICK-UP-*rock*

This discussion has reviewed the functions of classifiers and has described several ways to indicate plurality with singular or plural classifiers. It has also introduced the use of classifier handshapes in certain verbs to reflect various physical characteristics of the object. Further discussion of these features of ASL will occur in the *Text Analysis* and in other appropriate places elsewhere in this text.

G. Text Analysis

<pre>
                                          t   (gaze rt   )
Lee₁: (2h)"WELL" STUCK ME, ONE-DAY-PAST TIME⌣THREE, BROTHER brother(rt)-MEET-me
</pre>

<pre>
(gaze rt)nod   (gaze rt)
V:-CL@rt,out ⎱ 'sit facing each other',   CHAT"long time"
V:-CL@rt,in ⎰
</pre>

- **TIME⌣THREE**

    Notice in the illustration of this sign above that the hand-
    shape for the sign **THREE** is used while producing the
    sign **TIME**. This change makes the two signs look like a
    single sign. Thus, they are joined by the symbol ⌣ .

    (gaze rt   )
- *brother(rt)*-**MEET**-*me*

    This is an example of a conventional (widely used) sign in
    which classifier handshapes are used. In this sign, both
    hands use the '1' handshape 'person' classifier. The right
    hand **1-CL** (representing the 'brother') approaches the left
    hand **1-CL** (representing the Signer) from the right.

    (gaze rt   )nod
- **V:-CL@***rt,out*⎱ 'sit facing each other'
    V:-*CL@rt,in* ⎰

    This is an example of how the actions of two people can be
    presented by using a classifier on both hands. Notice that
    by positioning the two classifiers in a certain spatial ar-
    rangement, the Signer can indicate the spatial relation-
    ship between the brother and Lee. For further information
    about the locative uses of classifiers, see Units 6 and 15.

    (gaze rt)
- **CHAT**"*long time*"

    This is an example of a verb which has been modulated to
    indicate temporal aspect. This particular modulation usu-
    ally involves a slower and elliptical movement. However,
    with this particular verb, the movement is lengthened but
    not elliptical. For further information and discussion, see
    Units 8 and 17.

wh-q

Pat$_2$:   **BROTHER** *brother*-**MAKE-CONTACT-WITH**-*you* **FOR-FOR**

- *brother*-**MAKE-CONTACT-WITH**-*you*

  Notice that this verb is like the verbs ____-**JOIN-TO**-____ and ____-**BEAT-UP**-____. By changing the direction of movement of the dominant hand and the location of the non-dominant hand, it is possible to indicate both the subject and object. For more information on verbs like this, see Units 4 and 13.

(gaze rt)   t   puff.cheeks

Lee$_2$:   **INDEX**-*rt* **NEXT SUMMER, WANT _FAMILY FROM**-*rt*-**GROUP-COME-TO**-*here,*

neg

ME   NOT-WANT++ ,   US-TWO-*rt*   **STRUGGLE**"*regularly*"   **ALL-NIGHT**

- **_FAMILY**

  This is an initialized variant of the sign glossed as **CLASS** or **GROUP** which has become widely accepted. The sign is made with the following handshape on both hands.

  Some Signers will also use other initialized variants of this sign—e.g. the sign **_TEAM** is made by some Signers with the following handshape:

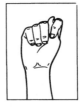

puff.cheeks

- **FROM**-*rt*-**GROUP-COME-TO**-*here*

  This is an example of how the classifier (2h)**C-CL**'group' can be moved as a verb. The sign moves from the right toward the Signer and means 'group come (from their home) to here'. Likewise, the same classifier could move away from the Signer and convey the meaning 'group go (from here) to ____'. For more information on this use of classifiers, see the *General Discussion* section above and Unit 5.

- **US-TWO**-*rt*

    This is an example of a plural pronoun in ASL. Because of the location in which it is produced, it is clear that it refers to the Signer and the Signer's brother. For further information, see Units 3 and 12.

- **STRUGGLE**"*regularly*"

    This is another example of a verb that is modulated to indicate temporal aspect. As the discussion in Unit 8 pointed out, the Signer's perception is important in determining when it is appropriate to use each modulation. In this case, the meaning is 'a lot' or 'repeatedly'.

- **ALL-NIGHT**

    This is an example of a time sign which indicates duration. For further information, see Unit 11.

						t

Pat₃: *me*-**PITY**-*you*,   **PAST   NIGHT   #CLUB   THUMB-INDEX**-*back rt*,

<u>(gaze rt   )puff.cheeks</u>   <u>(gaze rt)puff.cheeks</u>   <u>nodding</u>
(2h)alt.**MOVE**-*things-rt*,   **PAINT**-*rt-arc*   **CHANGE**-*rt-arc*   **FINE**wg

- *me*-**PITY**-*you*

    This is a directional verb that can indicate the subject and object by the direction of its movement. See Units 4 and 13 for further discussion.

<u>(gaze rt   )puff.cheeks</u>
- (2h)alt.**MOVE**-*things-rt*

    In this sign, the non-manual signal '*puff.cheeks*' conveys the meaning 'a lot' or 'a large number'. Thus, the Signer states that there was a lot of moving things around.

<u>(gaze rt)puff.cheeks</u>
- **PAINT**-*rt-arc*   **CHANGE**-*rt-arc*

    These are examples of verbs which indicate that the object is plural by means of an arc movement. See Units 7 and 16 for further discussion.
    Notice that the '*puff.cheeks*' signal with the sign **CHANGE**-*rt-arc* helps indicate that a lot of things were changed.

<u>   br   </u>
Pat₄: **KNOW   INDEX**-*lf thumb*   "**UMMM**"
     "***PSHAW***"

<u>(gaze rt) t</u>   <u>(nodding)t</u>
WALL-*rt*,   **PICTURE   STATE-SCHOOL   OLD   AWHILE-AGO**   (2h)alt.**C-CL**-*rt*'pictures on the wall',

                    <u>pursed lips   t</u>
(2h)alt.**TAKE-DOWN**-*pictures*   (2h)**BARE**-*wall*,   **WHITE, PAINT**-*wall*

_____(nodding)t
- (2h)alt.**C-CL**-*rt*'pictures on the wall'

    This is an example of the two-handed alternating move-
    ment that can be used with singular classifiers to indicate
    plurality (see Unit 5 and discussion above). The alternat-
    ing movement indicates that the pictures are located all
    over the wall, not in a particular order.

- (2h)alt.**TAKE-DOWN**-*pictures*

    Notice that since the objects of this verb (pictures) are
    somewhat randomly arranged on the wall, it is necessary
    for this verb to 'agree with' that arrangement. Thus, the
    two-handed alternating movement is also used with this
    verb.

_____pursed lips
- (2h)**BARE**-*wall*

    Notice that the non-manual signal *'pursed lips'* occurs
    with this sign. This signal has several meanings including
    the meaning 'smooth'. The *Text Analysis* section of Unit
    12 contains a brief discussion and photos of the *'pursed
    lips'* signal.

Lee$_4$:   **WHITE   YECCH**-*rt,*   **BETTER   GREEN   BETTER**

- **YECCH**-*rt*

    This sign is related to the sign **VOMIT.** However, this
    sign uses a sharp, single movement toward the thing that
    is detested. In this way, this verb can indicate the object
    by being produced in or toward the location of the object.

_____(gaze rt;   nodding)t
Pat$_5$:   **KNOW   INDEX**-*lf index*   **YOU   TROPHY   BOWLING**   (2h)**A-CL**-*rt"sweep in rows",*
         "PSHAW"

(gaze down)   (gaze rt,down   ) nodding
    BOX   (2h)alt.**PUT**-*trophies*-**IN**-*box*   **THROW-OUT**-*rt*

- **INDEX**-*lf index*

    This sign and the sign **INDEX**-*lf thumb* in Pat's fourth
    turn are examples of establishing referents on the non-
    dominant hand. See Unit 12 for further discussion.

- (2h)**A-CL**-*rt"sweep in rows"*

    This is an example of one way to indicate plurality with
    a singular classifier. For further information, see the *Gen-
    eral Discussion* section above.

- (2h)alt.-**PUT**-*trophies*-**IN**-*box*

    Notice that the two-handed alternating movement is used
    with this verb. This indicates that the trophies were put
    in the box one-by-one, but in no particular order.

<pre>
                                              nodding
       _____
Lee₅: #CLUB   CHANGE, IMPROVE* TRUE "HMMM"
</pre>

- **IMPROVE***

  Some Signers will indicate the extent or quantity of improvement by varying the distance which the dominant hand moves. Thus, to indicate a little improvement, the dominant hand might only move up to the wrist. In this case, a large degree of improvement is shown by moving the hand all the way up to the shoulder. (See the illustration.)

H. Sample Drills

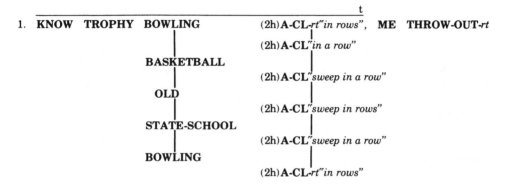

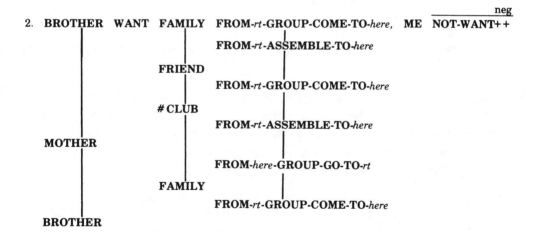

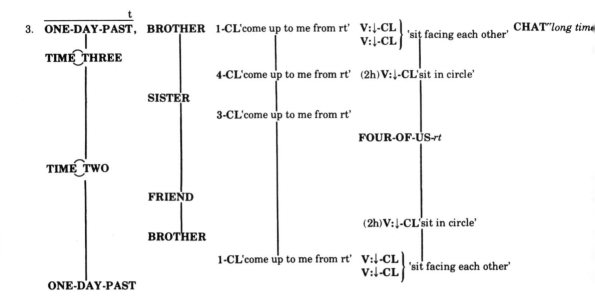

I. Video Notes

If you have access to the videotape package designed to accompany these texts, you will notice the following:

- In Pat's second turn, there is a particular non-manual signal which occurs with the sign **STRUGGLE**"*regularly*". This signal conveys the meaning 'again and again' and often implies that the action is 'hard'.

- Pat's use of his non-dominant (left) hand to list the activities that took place at the club (Pat$_4$ and $_5$).

- Pat's sign **PAINT**-*wall* is slightly different than the illustration in this unit. The sign illustrated above conveys the idea of painting with a small brush and, as such, is used more frequently when talking about painting things like pictures. The handshape used with this sign on the videotape is more appropriate when talking about painting large things like walls.

- Pat$_5$ provides a clear example of the "*sweep in rows*" modulation— (2h)**A-CL**"*sweep in rows*".

- When in the role of Addressee, Pat and Lee provide feedback to each other which shows their understanding and feelings. This feedback takes the form of head-nodding, changes in facial expression, and other non-manual behaviors.

Unit 15

Locatives

A. Synopsis

Pat and Lee are eating out. Pat asks if Lee remembers the girl that they were talking with yesterday. Lee asks if Pat means the short girl with freckles, and Pat says that's the one. She is hearing and her parents are Deaf and they live over by the residential school. Lee asks exactly where she lives. Pat says that she lives on the road that goes by the school—not far from the school. Lee asks what the girl does. Pat doesn't know, then remembers that she went to Chicago to look for a job. Lee asks how old she is. Pat thinks she is about twenty. Lee says that's really young.

B. Cultural Information: Hearing Children of Deaf Parents

It should not be surprising that the vast majority of deaf adults (85–90%) marry other deaf adults, rather than hearing adults. This type of intermarriage helps to provide a high degree of cohesiveness and continuity to the Deaf Community. What may seem surprising is that the vast majority of the children born to deaf parents have normal hearing. Although there has been very little study of these hearing children of deaf parents, there do seem to be some common experiences which many of them share. For example, many hearing children of deaf parents:

- —acquire signing skills before speaking skills. The type of signing skills they acquire depends on the type of signing that is used by the parents
- —are given the role of interpreter/transliterator for their parents at an extremely young age (often as young as five or six)
- —experience the pressures of participating in adult decisions (telephone calls, salespeople, etc.) at a very young age because of the interpreting or transliterating demands
- —go through a period of embarrassment because their parents are different and sign—which sometimes leads the child or adolescent to reject his/her parents and even refuse to sign in public
- —co-exist in two communities (the Deaf and the Hearing) and feel the need to become more deeply involved in each one

In 1979, the Registry of Interpreters for the Deaf (RID) published a small monograph entitled *Deaf Parents—Hearing Children*. This seems to be the only work currently available on this topic. The monograph describes the results of a survey of 300 hearing children of deaf parents and is available from the RID (814 Thayer Avenue, Silver Spring, Md. 20910).

C. Dialogue

Pat

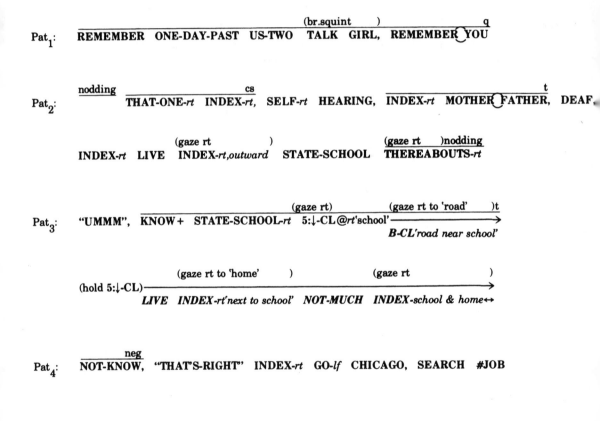

————————————————————————————————(br.squint   )————————————q
Pat₁: REMEMBER ONE-DAY-PAST US-TWO TALK GIRL, REMEMBER YOU

nodding ———————————————cs————————— ——————————————————t
Pat₂: THAT-ONE-*rt* INDEX-*rt*, SELF-*rt* HEARING, INDEX-*rt* MOTHER FATHER, DEAF,

              (gaze rt   )   (gaze rt)nodding
      INDEX-*rt* LIVE INDEX-*rt,outward* STATE-SCHOOL THEREABOUTS-*rt*

                            ——————————————(gaze rt)——— (gaze rt to 'road'   )t
Pat₃: "UMMM", KNOW+ STATE-SCHOOL-*rt* 5:↓-CL @*rt*'school'————————————→
                                                          B-CL'road near school'

              (gaze rt to 'home'   )   (gaze rt   )
      (hold 5:↓-CL)————————————————————————————————————→
              LIVE INDEX-rt'next to school' NOT-MUCH INDEX-school & home↔

          ———neg
Pat₄: NOT-KNOW, "THAT'S-RIGHT" INDEX-*rt* GO-*lf* CHICAGO, SEARCH #JOB

          ———neg
Pat₅: NOT-KNOW, FEEL AGE-TWENTY THEREABOUTS

Lee

Lee₁: <u>SMALL   GIRL   (2h)HAVE-FRECKLES-ON-*face*   THAT-ONE⁀ INDEX-*lf*</u>^q

Lee₂: <u>EXACT   WHERE   "WHAT"   EXACT</u>^{wh-q}
         OH-I-SEE

Lee₃: <u>(gaze lf)</u>   <u>wh-q</u>
         GIRL   #DO-DO   INDEX-*lf*
                                    "WHAT"

Lee₄: <u>AGE+   INDEX-*lf*</u>^{wh-q}
         OH-I-SEE

Lee₅: YOUNG   "WOW"

D. Key Illustrations

Pat

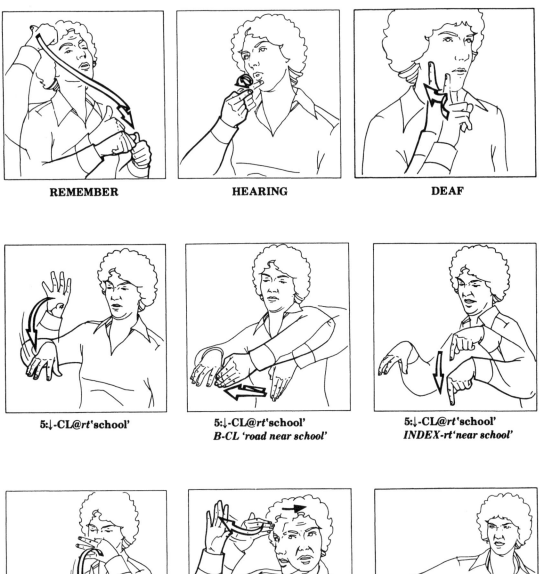

REMEMBER   **HEARING**   **DEAF**

5:↓-CL@*rt*'school'   5:↓-CL@*rt*'school'   5:↓-CL@*rt*'school'
                          B-CL 'road near school'   *INDEX-rt'near school'*

5:↓-CL@*rt*'school'   **NOT-KNOW**   **THEREABOUTS**
NOT-MUCH

Lee

| HAVE-FRECKLES-ON-*face* | "WHAT" | #DO-DO |

E. Supplementary Illustrations

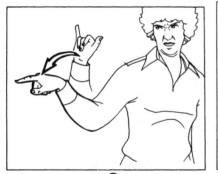

| THAT-ONE INDEX-*rt* | "THAT'S-RIGHT" | #JOB |

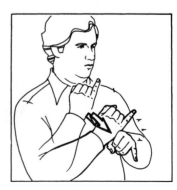

| OH-I-SEE | GO-*rt* | STATE-SCHOOL |

F. General Discussion: Locatives

The previous discussion of locatives (Unit 6) showed how Signers commonly use classifiers to indicate the spatial relationship between two or more things—where these things are in relation to each other. That discussion also touched on how certain verbs can be made at specific locations on the Signer's body to show where an action occurs (e.g. **HAVE-OPERATION-ON-____**), and, similarly, how other verbs can move from one spatial location to another to show where an action occurs (e.g. **FROM-____-FLY-TO-____**). This section will provide a further examination of these topics as well as describe ways that Signers use indexing or separate locative signs to indicate spatial relationships.

As stated in Unit 6, classifiers are frequently used to show spatial relationships because they can easily be moved around in space to reflect the actual arrangement of the things they represent. Thus, for example, the Signer can form a hill with the **'B'** handshape and then move the **'4→'** classifier along that 'slope' to indicate that there is a fence *on the side of* the hill.

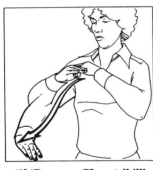
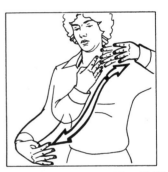

(2h)B_{outline}-CL-*cntr*'hill'   (2h)4→CL-*lf*'fence on side of hill'

Or, the Signer can use the **'V'** handshape classifier to represent a person who *stands on top of* the hill. Then the Signer might switch to the **'1'** handshape classifier and move it in a zig-zag manner downward to show the person *skiing down* the hill.

V-CL-*cntr*'stand atop hill'   1-CL-*cntr*'ski down hill'
B↓-CL-*cntr*'hill'

In the illustration above on the left, the spatial relationship between two things—the person and the hill—is indicated by positioning the two classifiers in that spatial relationship. That is, the **V-CL** is on top of the **B↓-CL**. But in the illustration on the right, the location of the hill is "remembered" (rather than represented with the non-dominant hand) and the **1-CL**'skier' moves downward along that remembered hill. Thus, in this case, the (changing) spatial relationship between the person and the hill is indicated by moving the classifier in the location which represents the hill.

"Remembering" locations is also important when describing the spatial relationship between more than two things. The Signer may be able to represent the relationship between two of those things by using a classifier on each hand, but the location of a third thing will need to be "remembered".

For example, suppose the Signer wants to describe what happened at a party. During that event, 'Pat' was sitting next to 'Lee' on Lee's left, and 'Fran' was sitting across from Pat. To describe the spatial relationship between these three people, the Signer would need to show the relationship between two of the people, "remember" that relationship, and then add the third person. Notice how Lee's location (1) is "remembered" in the illustration below.

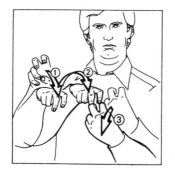

Another common way to indicate where something happens is to use a directional verb. Just as some classifiers can be moved as verbs in particular locations to show where something happens, directional verbs can move from one spatial location to another to indicate where an action occurs. This use of directional verbs occurred in several previous dialogues in which a place (e.g. a city, a store) was automatically assigned a spatial location and then all future references made use of that spatial location. Recall how the verbs **GO-TO-____** and **ASSEMBLE-TO-____** were used in Unit 10. Each of these verbs indicated movement toward a specific place which had been assigned a spatial location— **ASSEMBLE-TO**-*chicago*, **GO-TO**-*chicago*.

The two previous units on pronominalization (Units 3 and 12) described a strategy that ASL Signers frequently use to indicate the location of something—*indexing*. The Signer can index (point to) something actually present in the Signer's environment (e.g. a building), or the Signer can index a location in space which represents a person, thing, or place. In addition, just as two classifiers can be positioned next to each other to indicate a particular spatial relationship, the Signer sometimes will index a location around or on a classifier (made with the other hand) to indicate where something else is. Or, the Signer may index one location with one hand and index another location with the other hand to describe a spatial relationship.

For example, suppose the Signer wants to tell someone that New Jersey is 'right next to' and 'slightly below' New York. In this case, the Signer might assign a particular spatial location to New York with his/her right index finger and 'hold' that location by continuing to point at it. Then, using the left index finger, the Signer could indicate the relative location of New Jersey.

This type of indexing often occurs when the Signer is giving directions.

Since ASL generally uses the signing space to visually demonstrate locative relationships, it tends *not* to use separate locative signs to express these relationships in the way English uses prepositions. However, ASL does have several separate locative signs (e.g. **IN, ON, UNDER, OPPOSITE-FROM, NEAR, NEXT-TO, BETWEEN**) which are used in certain contexts. In general, these signs seem to be used when the Signer wants to focus on or emphasize the locative relationship. For example, suppose there are books all around, on, and under a table. If someone asks "Where's my book?", the Signer might respond:

$$\overline{\qquad\qquad\qquad t}\quad \text{(gaze lf}\qquad\qquad)\ \overline{\qquad\text{nodding}}$$
YOUR   BOOK,   TABLE   INDEX-*lf*   **ON-***lf*   **INDEX-***lf*

In addition, sometimes there is no classifier or directional verb in the sentence which could be used to specify an exact location. In these cases, a separate locative sign may be used. However, in general, ASL Signers use the signing space (using directional verbs, classifiers, or indexing) to indicate where things are and the locative relationship between those things.

G. Text Analysis

Lee₁: SMALL GIRL (2h)HAVE-FRECKLES-ON-*face* THAT-ONE͜ INDEX-*lf* ‾‾‾ᑫ

- **HAVE-FRECKLES-ON-*face***

    This is an example of a verb which can be made at a specific location on the Signer's body to show where something happens (like **HAVE-OPERATION-ON-___**). Thus, one could sign **HAVE-FRECKLES-ON-*arm*, HAVE-FRECKLES-ON-*nose*,** etc. Notice that this sign uses the '4:' classifier handshape, thus indicating plurality—i.e. there is more than one freckle on the face. For further information on signs of this type, see the *General Discussion* above and Unit 6.

- **THAT-ONE͜ INDEX-*lf***

    Notice that Lee produces this definite pronoun to the left, thus assigning that location to 'the small girl with freckles on her face'. And, in reality, that's where the girl was situated yesterday—to Lee's left—so Lee is following the *reality principle* described in Unit 3. For more information on definite pronouns, see Unit 12.

    Notice also that Lee's turn is a 'yes-no' question. Lee has answered Pat's question by describing the girl and asking if that's the girl Pat means.

Pat₂:
‾‾‾nodding‾‾‾‾‾‾‾‾‾‾‾‾‾‾‾‾‾cs‾‾‾‾‾‾‾‾‾‾‾‾‾‾‾‾‾‾‾‾‾‾‾‾‾‾‾‾‾‾‾‾‾‾‾‾‾t
THAT-ONE-*rt* INDEX-*rt*, SELF-*rt* HEARING, INDEX-*rt* MOTHER͜ FATHER, DEAF,

        (gaze rt   )   (gaze rt   )nodding
INDEX-*rt* LIVE INDEX-*rt,outward* STATE-SCHOOL THEREABOUTS-*rt*

-
        nodding ‾‾‾‾‾‾‾‾‾‾‾‾‾‾‾‾‾‾‾‾‾‾cs
    THAT-ONE-*rt* INDEX-*rt*

    Notice that Pat responds to Lee by nodding before beginning to sign. Notice also that the 'cs' signal which occurs with these signs refers to the relative distance between the girl and the two Signers, indicating that the girl was 'right there' close by.

-         (gaze rt   )
  LIVE   INDEX-*rt,outward*

    This is an example of how indexing is used to assign a spatial location. In this case, the location includes both where the parents live and the state school. Notice that by pointing outward (as well as to the right), Pat indicates that the location is some distance away from the Signers.

<u>(gaze rt   )nodding</u>
- **THEREABOUTS-*rt***

> This sign (which was discussed in Unit 11) can express either approximate time or approximate location. In this case, it is used to express the meaning that the girl's parents live somewhere around the state school.

wh-q

Lee₂: **EXACT WHERE "WHAT" EXACT**
    OH-I-SEE

> Notice that Lee, apparently not satisfied with an approximate location, asks Pat exactly where the girl's parents live—a 'wh-word' question. See Units 1 and 10 for a discussion of the non-manual behaviors for 'wh-word' questions.

Pat₃: **"UMMM", KNOW+ STATE-SCHOOL-*rt* 5:↓-CL@*rt*'school'—**
(gaze rt)   (gaze rt to 'road')t
B-CL'road near school'

(hold **5:↓-CL**)
     (gaze rt at 'home')   (gaze rt)
LIVE INDEX-rt'next to school' NOT-MUCH INDEX-school & home←→

- **5:↓-CL@*rt*'school'**

> Generally this classifier is used to represent a large house, mansion, city, etc. In this case, it represents the state school. Notice how the Signer holds this classifier for the rest of the turn, thus providing a point of reference for understanding where the home is located.

- **5:↓-CL@*rt*'school'**————————→
  B-CL'road near school'

> Notice in the illustration how the Signer shows that the 'road' is near or next to the 'school'—the **B-CL** moves back and forth close to the **5:↓-CL.** This is an example of how classifiers are used to indicate spatial relationships. However, if there were several roads next to the school (and thus Lee might not know which particular road), then Pat would have clearly identified the road by name or some other easily recognized description of the road.

- **5:↓-CL@*rt*'school'**————————→
  INDEX-next to school

> This is a good example of how the Signer can point to a spot on or around a classifier to indicate the relative location of something else. In this case, the Signer points to a spot near the state-school (**5:↓-CL@*rt***) to indicate the relative location of the home. See the *General Discussion* above for further information.

- *NOT-MUCH*

  This sign is generally used when discussing distance and, in that context, has the meaning 'not far'. However, it is also used when discussing quantities of things or prices of things. In these contexts, it has the meaning 'not much'. Perhaps a more general gloss such as **INSIGNIFICANT** could be used for this sign.

- 5:↓-CL@*rt*'school'————————————————→
                 INDEX-school & home←——→

  Notice that Pat refers to the area between the home and the school by moving the index finger back and forth between the classifier on the right hand (representing the school) and the location that Pat pointed to earlier (representing the home). With the previous sign, Pat indicates that the area is relatively small, that the school and home are not far apart.

<pre>
           (gaze lf)   wh-q
Lee₃: GIRL   #DO-DO   INDEX-lf
                                  "WHAT"
</pre>

- **#DO-DO**

  This is an example of a fingerspelled loan sign. In this context, it has the meaning 'what does the girl do?'. However, this fingerspelled loan can have several other meanings when its form is slightly changed. For example, if the hands are held with the palms down and move in small tandem circles, then the meaning is something like 'to do small chores'.

- **INDEX-*lf***

  Notice that Lee consistently uses the original location assigned to the girl—to Lee's left and Pat's right.

<pre>
             neg
Pat₅: NOT-KNOW, FEEL AGE-TWENTY THEREABOUTS
</pre>

<pre>
              neg
</pre>
- **NOT-KNOW**

  This is an example of *negative incorporation* which occurs with a small number of signs—**NOT-KNOW, NOT-WANT, NOT-LIKE,** and the sign **NOT-GOOD** which is usually glossed as **BAD.** Notice that these signs all have an outward twisting motion which negates the meaning of the sign they are based on. Compare the following signs:

KNOW	**NOT-KNOW**
WANT	**NOT-WANT**
LIKE	**NOT-LIKE**
GOOD	**NOT-GOOD**

- **AGE-TWENTY**

    This sign is similar to two signs that appeared in Unit 7—**AGE-SEVEN** and **AGE-THREE.**

AGE-SEVEN-rt   AGE-THREE-lf

H. Sample Drills

<pre>
                                        t   q
. SMALL GIRL HAVE-FRECKLES-ON-<i>face</i>,   THAT-ONE INDEX-<i>lf</i>
                     |
               HAVE-FRECKLES-ON-<i>arm</i>
                     |
               HAVE-OPERATION-ON-<i>heart</i>
                     |
               WASH-(AT)-<i>face</i>
                     |
               HAVE-OPERATION-ON-<i>upper arm</i>
                     |
               HAVE-FRECKLES-ON-<i>nose</i>
                     |
               WASH-(AT)-<i>hair</i>
                     |
               HAVE-OPERATION-ON-<i>forehead</i>
                     |
               HAVE-FRECKLES-ON-<i>face</i>
</pre>

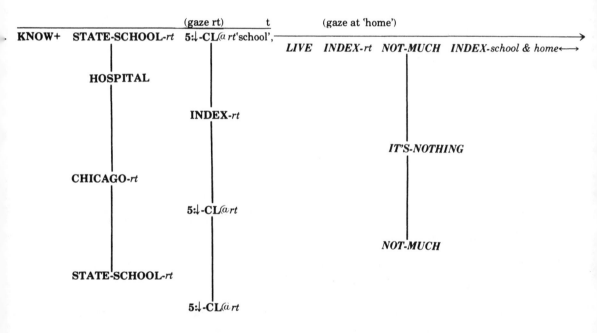

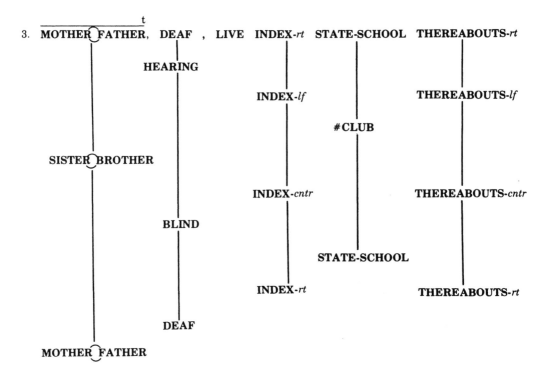

3.
$$\overline{\text{MOTHER FATHER, \quad DEAF \quad , \quad LIVE \quad INDEX-\textit{rt} \quad STATE-SCHOOL \quad THEREABOUTS-\textit{rt}}}^{\ \ t}$$

I. Video Notes

If you have access to the videotape package designed to accompany these texts, you will notice the following:

- Notice the non-manual signals 'q' (Pat₁ and Lee₁), 'wh-q' (Lee₂, Lee₃, and Lee₄), 'cs' (Pat₂), and 'neg' (Pat₄ and Pat₅).

- Lee constantly provides both manual **(OH-I-SEE)** and non-manual (head nods) feedback to Pat to indicate that she understands what Pat is saying.

- Pat₃ clearly illustrates how classifiers and indexing can be used to describe spatial relationships. Notice how the dominant hand classifier **(5:↓-CL-***rt***'**state school') serves as a reference point for describing the location of the street **(B-CL)** and where the girls' parents live **(*INDEX-rt'next to school'*)**.

- Notice in Pat's third turn how consistently his eye gaze indicates the relative location of each thing—the state school, the road, and the home.

Unit 16

Pluralization

A. Synopsis

Pat and Lee are co-workers who meet during their coffee break. Pat has just been talking with another co-worker about signed languages. Pat begins by calling Lee's attention to the girl who just left. Lee asks if Pat means the girl with the glasses. Pat says that's right and tells Lee what happened: the girl said that Sign Language is the same all over the world! Pat told her that there are different signed languages just as there are different spoken languages. Lee says that the girl doesn't know what she's talking about and reminds Pat about the World Federation of the Deaf meeting in 1975. There were a lot of Deaf people there and many different kinds of signing. Pat remembers that and describes how two Deaf people came over to talk, but s/he couldn't understand them because their signing was so different. Lee says that with all those Deaf people there, there should have been T.V. cameras recording their signing for later analysis. Pat also remembers the different interpreters. Lee remembers them, too. They were all lined up in front—one Spanish, one Russian, one French, twelve or thirteen of them altogether. Pat remembers how much fun it was looking at each one and seeing how different they were from each other. Lee says that signed languages are *not* all the same and that the girl is a nitwit!

B. Cultural Information: National Sign Languages and Gestuno

Contrary to what many people believe, Sign Language is not a universal language among Deaf people. This can be easily seen by examining books that illustrate signs from different countries like France, Australia, England, and Sweden; very often, different signs are used to represent the same thing. In addition, different signed languages often use different handshapes. For example, the handshape used in the ASL signs **FEEL** and **WHAT'S-UP** does not occur in Swedish signs; the handshape with the fourth finger extended is used in Taiwan signs (e.g. **SISTER**) but does not occur in any ASL signs. It is also reasonable to expect that there are differences in the grammar of different signed languages, but there has not yet been much research on this.

At international conferences and meetings, a common reaction of many hearing people is that because Deaf people from different countries seem to be able to communicate somewhat easily with each other, they must all be using the same Sign Language. However, several research studies have shown that this is not the case at all. In fact, according to Deaf people themselves, what happens is that they stop using their own Sign Language and instead use mime and gestures. This type of communication is generally slower than signing and involves much repetition and a constant give-and-take to figure out the meanings of various gestures. For more information on communication differences and difficulties with foreign Signers, there are two articles by Battison and Jordan in *Sign Language Studies 10* (1976). These articles report on some preliminary research done during the VII World Congress of the Deaf that was held in Washington, D.C. in 1975.

In 1975, the British Deaf Association (BDA) published a book entitled *Gestuno: International Sign Language of the Deaf* on behalf of the World Federation of the Deaf (WFD). This book contains photographs of approximately 1500 signs and represents an attempt at unifying the signed languages used by Deaf people. The signs shown in this book were selected by a committee that was set up by the WFD and that had one representative from each of the following countries: the United States, Great Britain, Russia, Denmark, and Italy. This committee relied on their own personal experience and knowledge as well as books of signs published in many countries. Their primary goal was to provide a quick and easy means of communication at international meetings of Deaf people.

In many ways, Gestuno is like Esperanto (an artificially devised spoken language intended to provide quick and easy communication among hearing people from different countries). However, Gestuno cannot be called a "language" for several reasons: first, it has no grammar (the book is simply a grouping of individual signs according to various topics); second, Gestuno has no native users (i.e. no children grow up using it as their first language); third, very few people are fluent in the use of Gestuno since there is little opportunity to practice or use it. Gestuno is not used by the Deaf people in any single country for daily, regular conversation; its use is restricted to international meetings.

It is highly unlikely that Gestuno will ever replace national signed languages even at international meetings. This is borne out by the fact that at the World Federation of the Deaf meeting in Bulgaria in 1979, each contingent of Deaf delegates and participants brought its own interpreters. In fact, many of the Deaf participants said that they felt cheated and only partially informed when they were forced to rely solely on Gestuno interpretation. Whether this was due to inadequate training and preparation of the Gestuno interpreters or the inadequacies and limitations of Gestuno itself, or both reasons, is not clear. In any case, just as Esperanto has not been widely accepted among hearing people, it is highly unlikely that Deaf people will replace their own Sign Language with Gestuno and that it will become universally accepted and used.

C. Dialogue

Pat

Pat₁:
<u>_____co</u>   <u>(gaze rt;_____cs)</u> <u>__t</u> <u>_____q</u>
"SHOULDER-TAP"   KNOW-THAT GIRL RECENT LEAVE-TO-*rt* INDEX-*rt*, KNOW+ YOU

Pat₂:
<u>(gaze rt____)_____nod</u>   <u>_____t</u>
THAT-ONE INDEX-*rt*, INDEX-*rt* NARRATE, SIGN LANGUAGE WORLD, (2h)SAME-ALL-OVE

       <u>(gaze rt) neg</u> <u>(gaze rt_____)</u>   <u>(gaze rt)</u>
ME ————————→ SIGN-*rt* LANGUAGE-*rt* DIFFERENT++-*rt-arc*
       "NO-NO"-*rt*

                                     <u>(gaze lf→rt_____)</u> <u>(gaze rt_____)</u>
(2h)*rt*-SAME-AS-*lf* SPEAK LANGUAGE-*lf* DIFFERENT++-*lf-arc* (2h)*rt*-SAME-AS-*lf* (2h)"WELL"

Pat₃:
       <u>_____t</u> <u>(gaze rt_____)</u>
YES+, DEAF TWO, 2-CL'come up to me', INDEX-*rt* SIGN DIFFERENT*,

<u>(gaze rt)_____neg</u>
  ME NOT UNDERSTAND INDEX-*rt*

Pat₄:
                 <u>_____q</u>
FINEwg, OTHER REMEMBER YOU INTERPRET DIFFERENT++-*rt-arc*

Pat₅: RIGHT YOU,

                            <u>(gaze rt at 'each interpreter'____)</u>
ME REMEMBER #FUN ME *me*-LOOK-AT-*interpreters"each"* DIFFERENT++-*rt-arc*

Lee

          (gaze lf) _____q
e₁: GIRL   (2h)GLASSES   THAT-ONE INDEX-*lf*

e₂: **GIRL   KNOW-NOTHING,**

_____
REMEMBER   W-F-D   AWHILE-AGO   NINETEEN   SEVEN   FIVE,

(nodding) (gaze cntr   )t
          DEAF   ASSEMBLE-TO-*cntr*,   SIGN   DIFFERENT+++-*arc*

                 (gaze lf _____)puff.cheeks
ee₃: **W-F-D   FINEwg,   DEAF   (2h)4-CL**'people mingle together',

                 (gaze lf & cntr↔   _____)br (gaze lf   )
        SHOULD   #TV   CAMERA-RECORD-*lf* & *cntr-arc*↔   FINISH,   ANALYZE++-*lf*

                 (gaze up,lf   )
ee₄: **YES+,   INTERPRET   (2h)4-CL-*up,lf*'**interpreters in a line,facing Signer',

(gaze up,lf   ) (gaze up,lf   ) (gaze up,lf cntr ‹   )
        SPAIN,   RUSSIA,   FRANCE,
INDEX-up,lf   *INDEX-up,lf* ———→   *INDEX-up,lf cntr* ———→

(gaze up,lf   ) (gaze down, 'thinking'   )
ALTOGETHER-*lf*   TWELVE+   THIRTEEN

_____rhet.q
ee₅: **SIGN   LANGUAGE   (2h)SAME-ALL-OVER,   NOT*,**

        GIRL   PEA-BRAIN*

D. Key Illustrations

Pat

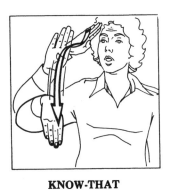

KNOW-THAT

NARRATE

(2h)SAME-ALL-OVER

2-CL'come up to me'

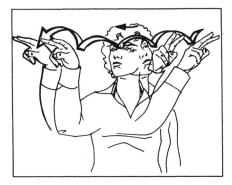

me-**LOOK-AT**-*interpreters"each"*

Lee

ASSEMBLE-TO-*cntr*   **DIFFERENT+++-*arc***   **(2h)4-CL'mingle'**

CAMERA-RECORD-*arc*

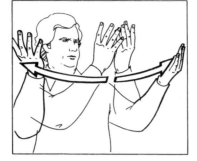

(2h)4-CL-*up,lf*
'interpreters in a line facing Signer'

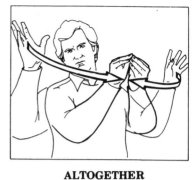

ALTOGETHER

NOT*

PEA-BRAIN*

E. Supplementary Illustrations

RECENT

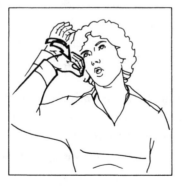

KNOW-NOTHING

INTERPRET+

F. General Discussion: Pluralization

Previous units have described a number of ways to indicate plurality—ways to show that there is more than one of something, for example with classifiers (Unit 14) or with pronouns (Unit 12). This discussion will provide additional information on some of the topics in these units. However, the focus of this discussion is how non-specific (indefinite) number signs are used and how verbs can also show that the subject or object is plural.

One way to indicate plurality is to repeat the noun (see Unit 7). However, this is possible with only a small number of signs (e.g. **ROOM/BOX, STATUE, AREA, RULE, HOUSE**) in certain contexts. It is generally true that repetition does *not* occur when a number sign is used with the noun unless the Signer wishes to assign spatial locations to each thing for later reference.

There are two general categories of number signs in ASL: specific number signs (e.g. **TWO, FIVE**) and non-specific number signs (e.g. **FEW, MANY**). In general, a specific number sign will occur *before* the noun (e.g. **TWO CHAIR**) unless the Signer wishes to focus on the number. When the Signer wishes to focus on the number, or when the number has special significance, then it is often signed *after* the noun (e.g. **CHAIR TWO***). Sometimes for emphasis, the number sign will occur both *before and after* the noun (e.g. **TWO CHAIR TWO***). When a number sign and a classifier refer to the same noun in a sentence, generally, the number sign will occur after the noun and the classifier will be last (e.g. **CAR FOUR 3→CL**"*in a row*"). In these cases, the classifier will 'agree with' the number sign. That is, the classifier will be repeated to indicate plurality, but not more times than specified by the number. For example, if the number sign is **FOUR,** the classifier will be repeated, but not made more than four times.

When it is not possible or necessary to specify an exact number, Signers may choose to use one of the non-specific (indefinite) number signs (**MANY, FEW, SEVERAL,** or **SOME/PART**). These non-specific number signs tend to occur after the noun and follow the other patterns of the definite number signs. However, they do not seem to be used as often in ASL as indefinite number words are used in a spoken language like English, perhaps because ASL has so many other ways of showing an indefinite plural (e.g. with classifiers).

The signs **SEVERAL** and **FEW** are similar except that more fingers are extended in the sign **SEVERAL** and it has a larger movement. The facial behaviors that usually occur with these signs also tend to be different. The sign **FEW** tends to occur with the *'pursed lips'* signal (indicating the 'smallness' of the number). The sign

SEVERAL may occur with several different facial behaviors. Two are illustrated below. Notice how the larger movement of the sign **SEVERAL** on the right and the *'puffed cheeks'* signal (which indicates a large number) 'agree' with each other.

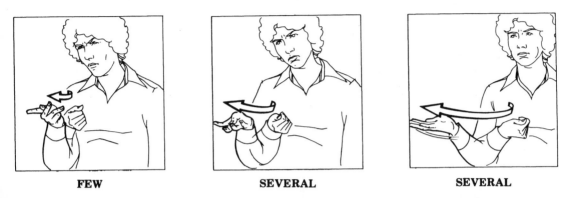

| FEW | SEVERAL | SEVERAL |

The sign **SOME/PART** seems to be used infrequently in ASL—although it occurs more often in English-influenced contexts. One context in which this sign may occur in ASL is when talking about dividing a large amount of money among several people—'some' to this person and 'some' to that person, etc.

Unit 8 described how verbs can be repeated or *modulated* in certain ways to indicate the duration or frequency of an event. However, verbs which are modulated in certain other ways will show that something is plural. For example, each of the verbs illustrated below indicate that something (either the subject or the object) is plural. You know that something is plural—

(a) when the verb is made in an arc

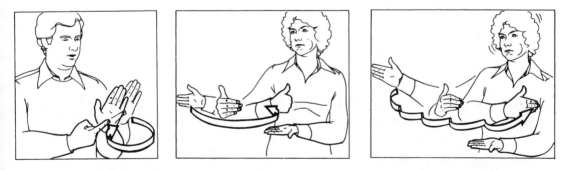

The modulations of these verbs indicate that the object is plural. The modulation (written as *"all"*) that occurs with the two verbs at the left and center is different from the modulation (written as *"each"*) that occurs with the verb on the right. The modulation on the right refers to a one-by-one "distribution" to or from each individual and will be described in Unit 18. The *"all"* modulation indicates a single action involving everyone or everything. However, both modulations involve an arc movement of the verb and signal that the object is plural.

(b) when both hands alternate
     (and move to or from different locations)

The verb on the left was seen in Unit 9 and described the act of 'arresting many people indiscriminately'. The same modulation occurs with the verb at center and also indicates that the object is plural (as in 'giving out something to many people'). The modulation shown on the right will be described in Unit 18.

(c) when both hands move at the same time
     to or from different locations in space

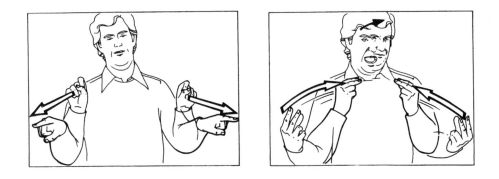

In the illustration on the left, each hand moves outward toward a separate location—indicating that two individuals or groups are the object of the verb _____-**ASK-TO-**_____. However, each hand moves *from* a separate location in the verb on the right—indicating that the subject is plural.

The various verb modulations illustrated and described above have different meanings and are used in different contexts. However, each of them includes the information that something is plural.

Some verbs in ASL always indicate that the subject is plural. Generally these verbs have a plural classifier handshape—i.e. the '4' or '5' handshape. Some of these

verbs have occurred in previous dialogues. Notice the plural classifier handshapes
in the following illustrations of verbs which always indicate a plural subject.

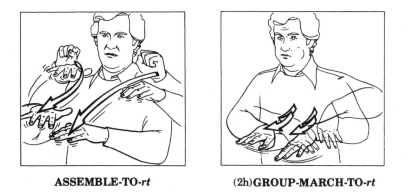

ASSEMBLE-TO-*rt*   (2h)GROUP-MARCH-TO-*rt*

This discussion has focused upon several strategies for indicating plurality in
ASL—including repetition of the noun, the use of specific and non-specific number
signs, and the use of various verb modulations. Examples of most of these strategies
have occurred in previous units and will be noted as they occur throughout the
remaining units.

G. Text Analysis

Pat₁:

<u>   co   </u>   <u>(gaze rt;   cs)</u>   <u>t</u>   <u>   q</u>

"SHOULDER-TAP" **KNOW-THAT GIRL RECENT LEAVE-TO**-*rt* **INDEX**-*rt,* **KNOW+** **YOU**

- <u>   co   </u>

  "SHOULDER-TAP"

  Notice that this is the first unit in which the *conversational opener* has involved physical contact. The main purpose of the conversational opener is to get the other person's attention. This is frequently done by waving a hand (**"HEY"**) at the other person. Sometimes the Signer will begin with a sign that will arouse the other person's attention and curiosity—like **AWFUL, DISGUSTING,** or **FINE**wg. In some contexts, lightly banging or tapping on a table creates vibrations which also will attract the other person's attention.

- <u>(gaze rt;   cs)</u>   <u>t</u>

  RECENT   LEAVE-TO-*rt*   **INDEX**-*rt,*

  Notice that the signs **LEAVE-TO**-*rt* and **INDEX**-*rt* not only indicate the direction in which the girl left, but also assign a location *(rt)* to the girl. Also notice how the *'cs'* signal occurs with both **RECENT** and **LEAVE-TO**-*rt,* meaning that the girl 'very recently' or 'just' left. (See Unit 11 for a discussion of the *'cs'* signal.)

Lee₁:

(gaze lf)   <u>   q</u>

      GIRL   (2h)GLASSES   THAT-ONE‿INDEX-*lf*

- **THAT-ONE‿INDEX**-*lf*

  Notice that Lee refers to the same spatial location given to the girl by Pat.

Pat₂:

<u>(gaze rt)   nod</u>   <u>   t</u>

THAT-ONE‿INDEX-*rt,* **INDEX**-*rt* **NARRATE,** **SIGN LANGUAGE WORLD,**

(2h)SAME-ALL-OVER,

<u>(gaze rt)neg</u> (gaze rt   )   (gaze rt)

ME⎯⎯⎯⎯⟶ **SIGN**-*rt* **LANGUAGE**-*rt* **DIFFERENT+ +**-*rt-arc*

     "NO-NO"-*rt*

                                 (gaze lf→rt   ) (gaze rt   )

(2h)rt-**SAME-AS**-*lf* **SPEAK LANGUAGE**-*lf* **DIFFERENT+ +**-*lf-arc* **(2h)**rt-**SAME-AS**-*lf* **(2h)"WEI**

- **(2h)SAME-ALL-OVER**

  Notice from the illustration above that this sign moves in an arc. This arc indicates that the subject is plural (see *General Discussion* section for more information). This sign is often used to express the meanings 'standard' or 'homogeneous'.

- **DIFFERENT+ + -*rt-arc***

    Notice how the Signer repeats the sign (+ +) in an arc to indicate plurality. This arc is produced in the location just assigned to signed languages (**SIGN**-*rt* **LANGUAGE**-*rt*), thus indicating that 'signed languages are different from each other'.

- (2h)*rt*-**SAME-AS**-*lf*

    This sign is used to equate two people, places, or things. Here the Signer equates signed languages (which have been assigned the location to the right) with something that will be assigned the location on the Signer's left. Thus, it would have been possible to gloss this sign as *signed languages*-**SAME-AS**-*lf*.

- **DIFFERENT+ + -*lf-arc***

    Again the Signer repeats the sign in an arc (in the location just assigned to spoken languages) to indicate plurality.

- *rt*-**SAME-AS**-*lf*

    Again the Signer equates what has been established on the right (signed languages) with what has been established on the left (spoken languages). Thus it would have been possible to gloss this sign as *signed languages-***SAME-AS**-*spoken languages.*

⠆   **GIRL   KNOW-NOTHING,**

REMEMBER   W-F-D   AWHILE-AGO   NINETEEN   SEVEN   FIVE,

(nodding) (gaze cntr   )t
⠀⠀⠀⠀⠀**DEAF   ASSEMBLE-TO**-*cntr,*   **SIGN   DIFFERENT+ + + -*arc***

- **DEAF**

    This sign is often used to refer to 'the Deaf Community' or 'Deaf people'.

- **ASSEMBLE-TO**-*cntr*

    This is an example of a sign which always indicates that its subject—in this case **DEAF**—is plural. Notice the plural classifier handshapes—(2h)**5↓wg**.

- **SIGN**

    This sign can be used as a verb or as a noun meaning 'signed language'.

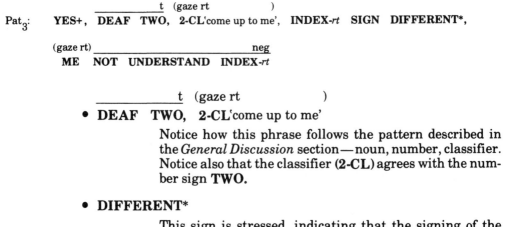

Pat₃:
_____t (gaze rt   )
YES+,   **DEAF TWO**,   **2-CL**'come up to me',   **INDEX**-*rt* **SIGN** **DIFFERENT***,

(gaze rt)_____neg
ME   **NOT**   **UNDERSTAND**   **INDEX**-*rt*

- _____t (gaze rt   )
  DEAF   **TWO**,   **2-CL**'come up to me'

   Notice how this phrase follows the pattern described in the *General Discussion* section—noun, number, classifier. Notice also that the classifier (**2-CL**) agrees with the number sign **TWO**.

- **DIFFERENT***

   This sign is stressed, indicating that the signing of the two people was *very* different.

Lee₃:
(gaze lf   _____)puff.cheeks
W-F-D **FINEwg**,   **DEAF**   (2h)**4-CL**'people mingle together',

(gaze lf & cntr⟷   )br   (gaze lf   )
SHOULD **#TV** **CAMERA-RECORD**-*lf & cntr-arc*⟷   **FINISH**,   **ANALYZE++**-*lf*

- (2h)**4-CL**'people mingle together'

   This is another example of a verb which indicates that its subject is plural. Again notice the plural classifier handshapes.

- **CAMERA-RECORD**-*lf & cntr-arc*⟶

   Notice how the arc indicates that the object (Deaf people mingling) is plural. The double headed arrow ⟷ means that the sign moves back and forth.

Lee₄:
(gaze up,lf   )
YES+,   **INTERPRET**   (2h)**4-CL**-*up,lf*'interpreters in a line,facing Signer',

(gaze up,lf   ) (gaze up,lf   ) (gaze up,lf cntr   )
       SPAIN,   **RUSSIA**,   **FRANCE**,
INDEX-*up,lf*   *INDEX*-*up,lf* ⟶   *INDEX*-*up,lf cntr* ⟶

(gaze up,lf   ) (gaze down,'thinking'   )
ALTOGETHER-*lf*   **TWELVE+**   **THIRTEEN**

- (2h)**4-CL**-*up,lf*'interpreters in a line,facing Signer'

   This classifier provides several pieces of information: (the subject is plural)—there were many interpreters; the interpreters were arranged in a line, and they were facing the Signer (who, presumably, was in the audience).

| | SPAIN, | RUSSIA, | FRANCE |

• *INDEX-up,lf*   *INDEX-up,lf*————→   *INDEX-up,lf,cntr*————→

Notice how the Signer points with the left hand to assign
a spatial location to each interpreter. This left hand index
is held while the right hand produces the sign **RUSSIA**
(which is normally a two-handed sign) and then held again
while the other hand signs **FRANCE.**

Pat₅: **RIGHT   YOU,**

(gaze rt at 'each interpreter'   )

ME   REMEMBER   #FUN   ME   *me-***LOOK-AT-***interpreters"each"*   **DIFFERENT++-***rt-arc*

• *me-***LOOK-AT-***interpreters"each"*

Once again the Signer uses an arc which indicates that
the object is plural. Notice that the sign ____-**LOOK-AT-**
____ is repeated at several places along the arc. This verb
modulation is written as *"each"* and indicates that there
were repeated actions of the same kind (i.e. repeated 'looking'). Because the verb points toward locations that were
previously assigned to 'interpreters', it is clear what the
Signer was looking at. For more information on the modulation *"each"*, see Unit 18.

• **DIFFERENT++-***rt-arc*

This sign is also repeated in an arc. By being made in the
locations assigned to the interpreters, this sign indicates
that the interpreters the Signer was looking at were different.

rhet.q

Lee₅: _____
        SIGN   LANGUAGE   (2h)SAME-ALL-OVER,   NOT*,

        GIRL   PEA-BRAIN*

rhet.q

• **SIGN   LANGUAGE   (2h)SAME-ALL-OVER**

This is an example of a rhetorical question. See Unit 10 for
a description of the non-manual behaviors used with
rhetorical questions. Again, notice that the sign
(2h)SAME-ALL-OVER uses an arc to indicate plurality.

H. Sample Drills

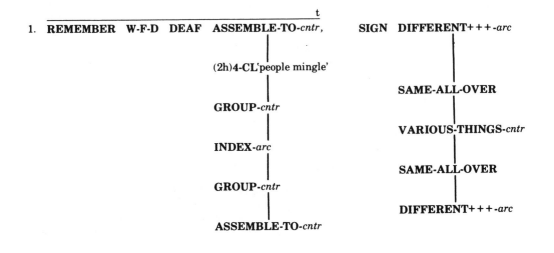

$$\overline{\rule{0pt}{1em}\hspace{12em}}^{\,t}$$

1. REMEMBER W-F-D DEAF ASSEMBLE-TO-*cntr*,   SIGN DIFFERENT+++-*arc*

(2h)4-CL'people mingle'

GROUP-*cntr*   SAME-ALL-OVER

INDEX-*arc*   VARIOUS-THINGS-*cntr*

GROUP-*cntr*   SAME-ALL-OVER

ASSEMBLE-TO-*cntr*   DIFFERENT+++-*arc*

$$\overline{\rule{0pt}{1em}\hspace{18em}}^{\,q}$$

2. FINEwg, OTHER REMEMBER YOU INTERPRET DIFFERENT++-*rt-arc*

me-**LOOK-AT**-*interpreters"each"*

CAMERA-RECORD-*rt & cntr-arc*⟵⟶

(2h)alt.1-**CL**'come up to me'

ASSEMBLE-TO-*cntr*

(2h)4-**CL**'in a row facing Signer'

(2h)4-**CL**'people mingle'

DIFFERENT++-*rt-arc*

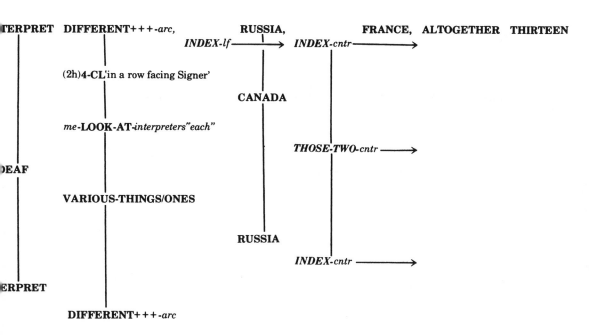

I. Video Notes:

If you have access to the videotape package designed to accompany these texts, you will notice the following:

- In Pat's first turn, notice that she gets Lee's attention by simply putting her hand on his arm and leaving it there until he looks up.

- In Pat's second turn when she is explaining what the girl said, she "role plays" the girl with an obvious note of sarcasm.

- In Lee's second turn, he tightens his closed lips while signing **SIGN DIFFERENT+++-*arc*.** This behavior frequently occurs with *assertions* — statements which assert that something is true.

- Lee's third turn provides a clear example of the *'puff.cheeks'* signal (used with the (2h)**4-CL).**

- Lee's final turn begins with a rhetorical question. Notice the non-manual signal *'rhet.q'* in the one-shot view of Lee.

Unit 17

Temporal Aspect

A. Synopsis

Pat and Lee are co-workers in an office who meet during their coffee break. Pat asks Lee what's happening. Lee says nothing's new, just the same old thing. Pat says that's how it is with him/her and suggests that they go to a movie together on Saturday. Lee can't because his/her parents are going away for the weekend and s/he has to take care of his/her brother. Pat asks Lee how old that brother is. Lee says he is eight and bothers Lee all the time. Lee's really had it with him. Pat asks whether Lee's brother likes to watch television. Lee replies that he watches it all morning on Saturday, but doesn't understand what is being said and is always asking Lee what they're saying. Lee wishes they would have people who can sign on television or have an interpreter. Pat says they have that on a television program called "Rainbow's End". Apparently all the people on that program are Deaf, and they sign in ASL. Pat says s/he watched it and really laughed again and again because it was so good. Lee says that s/he hasn't seen it yet but should see it.

B. Cultural Information: Rainbow's End

In January, 1979, a five-part television series entitled "Rainbow's End" was aired nationally on PBS. This creative new series is like Sesame Street—except that it is designed for Deaf children, their families, and their teachers. The series focuses on the amusing antics of a special group of characters (almost all of whom are Deaf) who work in a TV studio. The program was funded by the Bureau of Education for the Handicapped and was produced by D.E.A.F. Media, Inc., a non-profit California-based organization.

The overall goals of this series are: to provide positive role models—adult and peer—for Deaf children; to facilitate the development of English and reading; to foster family and classroom interaction; and to develop an awareness of the language and culture of Deaf people. To accomplish these goals, there are regular segments in each show: for example, "Famous Deaf Adults" from the past and present; dramatized stories and humorous situations; visits by "Supersign" who provides opportunities for learning helpful signs; and Deaf Awareness segments which provide some cultural information about the Deaf Community.

In general, the five-part series is presented in American Sign Language with voice-over narration. In addition, because of the educational goals of the program, each show is captioned. Future shows in the "Rainbow's End" series are planned and, hopefully, will soon be available. For more information write: D.E.A.F. Media, Inc., 401 E. 21st Street, Oakland, Ca. 94606.

C. Dialogue

Pat

Pat₁: <u>co</u>   <u>wh-q</u>
          "HEY",   WHAT'S-UP

Pat₂: *me*-SAME-AS-*you*+, SATURDAY <u>WHY NOT US-TWO GO-TO-*rt* (gaze rt   )   wh-q MOVIE</u>

Pat₃: <u>   wh-q</u>
          AGE+ INDEX-*brother*

Pat₄: <u>   neg+q</u>
          BROTHER NOT-LIKE LOOK-AT-*cntr* #TV

Pat₅: <u>nodding</u>   <u>   t</u>
          FINISHwg, #TV NAME, R-A-I-N-B-O-W'-S E-N-D,

          SEEM #ALL-*arc* PEOPLE DEAF, <u>nodding</u>
                                            SEEM+,

          SIGN CONVERSE-IN-ASL, <u>(gaze down,cntr   )</u>
                                   ME *me*-LOOK-AT-*tv* BELLY-LAUGH*"over & over again"*,

          GOOD INDEX-*tv* WOW

Lee

Lee₁: (2h)NOTHING $\overline{\text{SAME-OLD-THING}}^{\text{nodding}}$

Lee₂: $\overline{\text{CAN'T STUCK,}}^{\text{neg}}$ $\overline{\text{MOTHER͡FATHER,}}^{\text{t}}$ GO-*lf*

    (gaze lf   )
    (2h)SATURDAY͡SUNDAY *parents*-TELL-TO-*me* TAKE-CARE-OF BROTHER INDEX-*rt*

Lee₃: (2h)"WELL" AGE EIGHT,   INDEX-*rt* $\overline{\text{EVERY-DAY,}}^{\text{t}}$
                                "WELL"

    brother-BOTHER-*me*"*regularly*" ME SICK-OF͡INDEX-*rt*

Lee₄: (2h)"WELL", $\overline{\text{SATURDAY ALL-MORNING,}}^{\text{t}}$ INDEX-*brother* $\overline{\text{(2h)}brother\text{-LOOK-AT-}tv(\text{lf})"over time",}}^{\text{(gaze down,lf}\qquad\qquad\text{)mm}}$

    $\overline{\text{PROBLEM,}}^{\text{rhet.q}}$ $\overline{\text{INDEX-}brother\ \text{NOT}}^{\text{(gaze rt}\qquad\text{)}}$ $\overline{\text{UNDERSTAND}\ \overline{\text{INDEX-}lf}^{\text{(gaze lf)}}\ \text{SPEAK,}}^{\text{neg}}$

    (2h)"WELL", INDEX-*brother* ALWAYS *brother*-ASK-TO-*me*

    (body shift rt,gaze up lf   )
        INDEX-*tv* SAY #TV SAY INDEX-*tv*, ME "PSHAW",

    $\overline{\text{WISH}\quad\text{#TV}}^{\text{br}}\quad\overline{\text{INDEX-}tv\qquad\qquad\text{SIGN,}\quad\text{INTERPRET,}\quad\text{SOMETHING}}^{\text{(gaze lf}\quad\text{puff.cheeks}\qquad\qquad\text{)}}\quad\overline{\text{WISH*}}^{\text{nod}}$

Lee₅: FINEwg, $\overline{\text{ME NOT-YET SEE INDEX-}tv,}^{\text{neg}}$ $\overline{\text{SHOULD+}\quad\text{ME}}^{\text{rapid nodding}}$

D. Key Illustrations

Pat

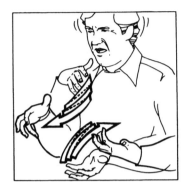

me-SAME-AS-*you*   BELLY-LAUGH*"over & over again"*   WOW

Lee

(2h)NOTHING   *parents*-TELL-TO-*me*   *brother*-BOTHER-*me"regularly"*

SICK-OF○INDEX-*rt*   *brother*-ASK-TO-*me*

$\overline{\hspace{3cm}}$ neg
UNDERSTAND

SOMETHING/SOMEONE

FINEwg

NOT-YET

E. Supplementary Illustrations

GO-*rt*

WHY NOT

NOT-LIKE

SAME-OLD-THING

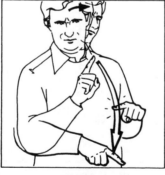

CAN'T

FINISHwg

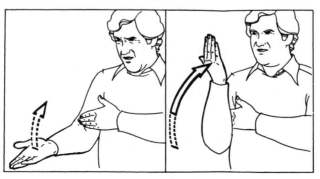

ALL-MORNING

E. General Discussion: Temporal Aspect

The previous discussion of temporal aspect in ASL (Unit 8) described two modulations that are used with verbs to convey information about the duration or frequency of an action. The first modulation *("regularly")* indicates that the action occurs frequently or a lot. This modulation usually has a repeated, small straight-line movement.

me-**LOOK-AT**-*something"regularly"*

Another modulation described in Unit 8 *("long time")* indicates that, from the Signer's perspective, the action lasted for a long time. This modulation has a slower, repeated elliptical movement.

me-**LOOK-AT**-*something"long time"*

A third modulation was mentioned briefly in the *Text Analysis* of Unit 8. This modulation indicates that something happens 'for awhile', 'continually', or 'regularly'. It has a repeated, circular movement and is written as *"over time"*.

me-**LOOK-AT**-*something"over time"*

Signers often use this modulation when they view the action as normal or routine. Suppose, for example, that a little boy's pet turtle died yesterday and when he found the dead turtle, the boy cried for about an hour. When describing what happened yesterday, the boy's sister might say that her brother 'cried for awhile'. In this case, she views the action (her brother's period of crying) as appropriate and normal.

CRY"*over time*"

Remember that modulations for temporal aspect do not indicate how long something actually lasts, but how the Signer feels about that length of time. So two people might describe the same event differently. For example, in the situation described above, the little boy's brother might feel that the boy had cried for too long a period of time, or 'for a long time'.

CRY"*long time*"

There is another modulation which indicates that something happens unusually often, with a period of time between each repetition of the event. Often this movement is used when the Signer has a negative feeling about the event—like having to do something again and again that is hard or unpleasant to do. This modulation is written as "*over & over again*". It is made with a tense straight-line movement (with a 'hold' at the end of each 'thrust' and an arc-like return to the starting place) and a forward rocking motion of the body and/or head with each thrust. The manual movement of the "*over & over again*" modulation is illustrated below.

For example, suppose there's an abstract painting on the wall. During the past several days, the Signer has repeatedly walked over to it and studied it, struggling to understand what the artist was trying to convey. The Signer's struggle to understand and repeated viewing of the painting over a period of time could be expressed with the "*over & over again*" modulation (and appropriate facial behavior).

me-LOOK-AT-*painting*"*over & over again*"

Similarly, suppose the Signer has to work on several projects during the course of a week. But there is one particular project that s/he has really worked hard on for over a month now. That repeated intense focus on the same project could be expressed by signing

WORK"*over & over again*"

Thus far, we have described four modulations for temporal aspect—movements which indicate the Signer's perception of the duration or frequency of an event. These are:

"*over time*"

"*regularly*"

"*long time*"

"*over & over again*"

These modulations most frequently occur with verbs. However, as you will learn later, some of them may be used with other types of signs.

G. Text Analysis

Lee$_1$:
<pre>
                        nodding
        (2h)NOTHING SAME-OLD-THING
</pre>

- **SAME-OLD-THING**

    Notice how the movement of this sign is repeated. This sign can be made with the *"over time"*, or *"long time"*, or *"over & over again"* modulation. The Signer's perception of the 'routine' will determine which modulation s/he chooses to use.

Pat$_2$:
<pre>
                                      (gaze rt   )   wh-q
  me-SAME-AS-you+, SATURDAY WHY NOT US-TWO GO-TO-rt MOVIE
</pre>

- *me*-**SAME-AS**-*you*

    This sign is similar to the pronoun **US-TWO** in that it moves back and forth between two people or things, or between the spatial locations assigned to two people or things.

Lee$_2$:
<pre>
            neg   t
   CAN'T STUCK, MOTHER FATHER, GO-lf
</pre>

<pre>
(gaze lf   )
(2h)SATURDAY SUNDAY parents-TELL-TO-me TAKE-CARE-OF BROTHER INDEX-rt
</pre>

- **(2h)SATURDAY SUNDAY**

    This sign is another example of two signs produced in such a way that they look like a single sign. This sign can be made with one or two hands. It is produced by starting with the sign **SATURDAY** (palm facing the Signer) and then twisting the hand(s) outward while opening to form the sign **SUNDAY**. The meaning of this combination is 'weekend'.

Lee$_3$:
<pre>
                                         t
   (2h)"WELL" AGE EIGHT,   INDEX-rt EVERY-DAY,
                          "WELL"
</pre>

<pre>
  brother-BROTHER-me"regularly" ME SICK-OF INDEX-rt
</pre>

- **EVERY-DAY**

    This sign expresses the concept of regularity (see Unit 11). It does not necessarily mean that something occurs every single day. Rather, the action occurs frequently or regularly enough that it seems to the Signer as if it happens every day. Likewise, in English, someone could say 'Pat bothers me all the time' even though Pat often is not even around; it just seems like it is 'all the time'.

- *brother*-**BOTHER**-*me"regularly"*

  > This is a directional verb which indicates both the subject and the object via its movement and location. (See Units 4 and 13). Notice that the modulation called *"regularly"* also occurs with this verb and indicates that the action occurs a lot or frequently. For further discussion of this particular movement, see Unit 8.

Pat₄:

	neg+q		
BROTHER	**NOT-LIKE**	**LOOK-AT**-*cntr*	**#TV**

> Notice that Pat combines the 'negation' and 'yes-no' question signals together to make this sentence a negated question. These signals are described in Units 1 and 10. Examine the photograph below to see what this combined signal looks like.

neg+q
NOT

e₄:

	t		(gaze down,lf	)mm
(2h)**"WELL"**,	**SATURDAY**	**ALL-MORNING**,	**INDEX**-*brother*	(2h)*brother*-**LOOK-AT**-*tv*(lf)*"over time"*,

	rhet.q	(gaze rt)		(gaze lf)	neg
PROBLEM,	**INDEX**-*brother*	**NOT**	**UNDERSTAND**	**INDEX**-*lf*	**SPEAK**,

(2h)**"WELL"**, **INDEX**-*brother* **ALWAYS** *brother*-**ASK-TO**-*me*

(body shift rt,gaze up lf	)
INDEX-*tv* **SAY #TV SAY INDEX**-*tv*, **ME "PSHAW"**,

	br	(gaze lf	puff.cheeks	)		nod
WISH #TV	**INDEX**-*tv*		**SIGN**,	**INTERPRET**,	**SOMETHING**	**WISH***

- **ALL-MORNING**

  > This is an example of a time sign which is used to indicate duration. See Unit 11 for further discussion of signs which indicate duration.

(gaze down,lf   )mm

- (2h)*brother*-**LOOK-AT**-*tv(lf)"over time"*

  This is another example of a directional verb made with a modulation which conveys information about time. This particular modulation indicates that the action continues for a normal or regular period of time (which in this case is 'all morning').

  The fact that this is a normal or regular event is conveyed by the non-manual adverb written as *'mm'*. When this adverb is used with a verb, it indicates that the action is 'normal' or 'regular', or that 'things are going along fine, as expected'. The *'mm'* signal is shown in the following two photographs.

_mm_   _mm_
DRIVE   **WRITE**

                 rhet.q
- **PROBLEM**

  This is an example of a rhetorical question. Notice that it is not a true question since Lee does not wait for Pat to answer. For a description of the non-manual signal used with rhetorical questions, see Unit 10.

                                         (gaze lf   )   neg
- **NOT　UNDERSTAND　INDEX**-*lf*　**SPEAK**

  Notice that the Signer has chosen to use a separate sign of negation (**NOT**) in this sentence even though the *'neg'* signal alone with the sign **UNDERSTAND** would convey the meaning 'don't understand'.

- *brother*-**ASK-TO**-*me*

  This is another example of a directional verb which indicates its subject and object. Here the sign moves from the brother's location on Lee's right toward the Signer (Lee).

(body shift rt, gaze up lf   )
-    **INDEX**-*tv*   **SAY　#TV　SAY　INDEX**-*tv*

  This is an example of what has been called *role playing* or *direct address*. Here the Signer assumes the role of the younger brother in order to quote the younger brother's comments. Notice that when the Signer assumes this role, his/her body leans to the right and s/he looks upward—as if talking to someone older and taller. When the Signer is finished quoting the younger brother, the Signer's body stance and eye gaze returns to normal.

Pat₅:
<u>nodding</u>   <u>t</u>
FINISHwg, #TV NAME, R-A-I-N-B-O-W-'S E-N-D,

                           <u>nodding</u>
SEEM #ALL-*arc* PEOPLE DEAF, SEEM+,

                     (gaze down,cntr   )
SIGN CONVERSE-IN-ASL,   ME *me*-LOOK-AT-*tv* BELLY-LAUGH"*over & over again*",

GOOD INDEX-*tv* WOW

- **FINISHwg**

  This is a variant of the sign **FINISH.** It is often used when responding to a question. Here the sign has a matter-of-fact tone, indicating that what Lee wishes has already happened.

- **#ALL-*arc***

  This is an example of a fingerspelled loan sign. Notice that the sign moves in an arc to indicate plurality.

- **BELLY-LAUGH"*over & over again*"**

  The sign **BELLY-LAUGH** is used to describe a type of 'laughing' that is more intense than the type described with the sign **LAUGH.** Compare the illustration of **BELLY-LAUGH"*over & over again*"** with the following illustration of the sign **LAUGH.**

LAUGH

Notice also that the "*over & over again*" modulation occurs with this sign in the dialogue. However, with this sign, the 'arc-like return' after each 'thrust' does not occur. (Compare the illustration of this sign with illustrations of the same modulation with two other verbs in the *General Discussion*.) The sign **BELLY-LAUGH** is like the verb **CHAT;** both of these signs normally do not have an arc-like return to the starting place after each thrust when they are modulated for temporal aspect.

H. Sample Drills

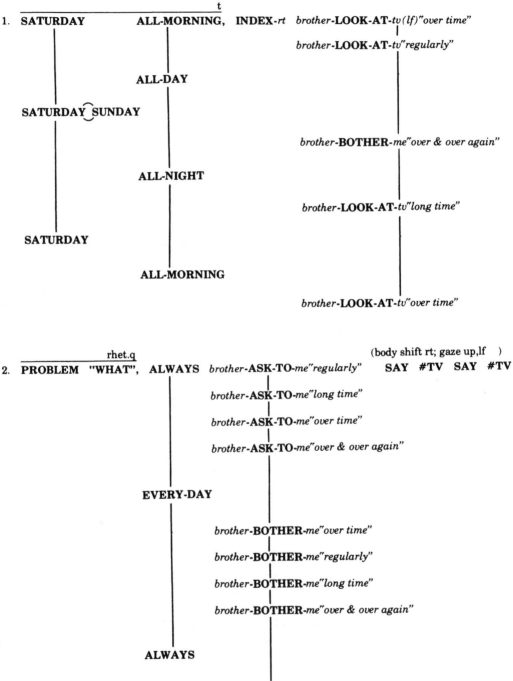

1. SATURDAY   ALL-MORNING,   INDEX-*rt*   *brother*-**LOOK-AT**-*tv (lf)*"*over time*"

brother-**LOOK-AT**-*tv*"*regularly*"

ALL-DAY

SATURDAY SUNDAY

brother-**BOTHER**-*me*"*over & over again*"

ALL-NIGHT

brother-**LOOK-AT**-*tv*"*long time*"

SATURDAY

ALL-MORNING

brother-**LOOK-AT**-*tv*"*over time*"

rhet.q   (body shift rt; gaze up,lf)

2. PROBLEM "WHAT", ALWAYS *brother*-**ASK-TO**-*me*"*regularly*"   SAY #TV SAY #TV

brother-**ASK-TO**-*me*"*long time*"

brother-**ASK-TO**-*me*"*over time*"

brother-**ASK-TO**-*me*"*over & over again*"

EVERY-DAY

brother-**BOTHER**-*me*"*over time*"

brother-**BOTHER**-*me*"*regularly*"

brother-**BOTHER**-*me*"*long time*"

brother-**BOTHER**-*me*"*over & over again*"

ALWAYS

brother-**ASK-TO**-*me*"*regularly*"

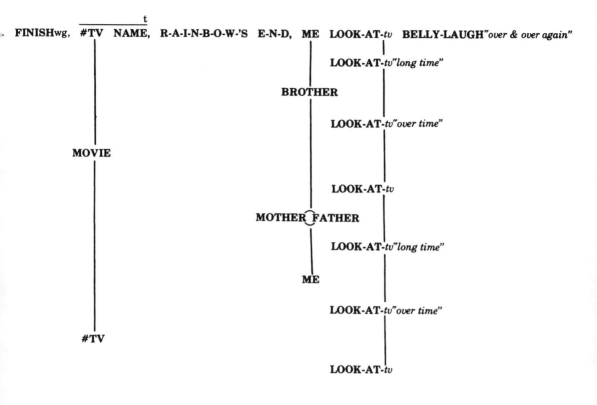

I. Video Notes

If you have access to the videotape package designed to accompany these texts, you will notice the following:

- Notice the *"over time"* modulation with the sign **SAME-OLD-THING** in Lee's first turn.

- Notice how the sign (2h)**SATURDAY⌒SUNDAY** is produced in Lee's second turn. This sign can also be made with one hand.

- In Lee's fourth turn, he uses a particular non-manual signal with the sign (2h)*brother-***LOOK-AT-***tv(lf)"over time"* that indicates that the action was 'normal; as expected; or regular'. Observe how this facial adverb is made during the dialogue and compare it with the two photographs in the *Text Analysis* section.

- Notice that in Lee's fourth turn he "role plays" his brother. This is indicated by Lee's body shift and his eye gaze. In effect, Lee is quoting his brother.

- During Pat's fifth turn, Lee provides feedback with the sign **FINE**wg which is repeated several times.

- The one-shot of Lee provides an excellent view of the *"regularly"* and *"over time"* modulations.

- In Pat's fourth turn, two non-manual signals (*'neg'* and *'q'*) are used simultaneously. Look at the one-shot view to see how these two signals look when they occur together.

Unit 18

Distributional Aspect

A. Synopsis

Pat and Lee meet outside a building on their way to lunch. Pat asks about Lee's plans for next Saturday. Lee hasn't decided yet and asks Pat what's going on. Pat explains that the club is showing a movie in which one of the actors signs. Lee asks if the actor is Deaf. Pat doesn't know but says s/he will ask several people on Saturday and find out. Lee reminds Pat of a movie (but can't remember the name) that had two actors signing in it. But those two actors were hearing. Pat remembers and recalls that the company bought some tickets and was trying to give them away free. Lee says that Deaf people all over the U.S. got mad and sent letters of complaint to the company. The company finally had enough and decided that in the future if a movie called for signing or a Deaf person, they would ask around and hire a real Deaf person. Pat says that maybe the movie Saturday night will have a Deaf actor. Lee doesn't think so and says that if the actor is Deaf, s/he will give everybody a dollar.

B. Cultural Information: Deaf Actors and Actresses

In March, 1979, a special preview of the MGM film "Voices" was held in San Francisco. The film portrays a love story about a Deaf woman who aspires to be a dancer and who falls in love with a hearing man. The role of the Deaf woman was portrayed by a hearing actress. For many Deaf actors and actresses in California, this brought to focus many years of frustration and anger at being denied roles in movies and on television. Consequently, a "Coalition Against Voices" was formed to protest such discrimination. On April 6, 1979, a demonstration was held at the San Francisco premier of the film. This demonstration was one more attempt to sensitize those in the television and film industry toward the type of discrimination that Deaf artists have been enduring for so many years.

Ironically, while the film "Voices" demonstrates that a Deaf person *can* be a dancer, the film and television industry have felt that a Deaf person *cannot* be an actor and have consistently chosen hearing actors to portray Deaf roles—for example, "Dummy", "The Miracle Worker", "Airport '79", "Mom and Dad Can't Hear Me", etc. A notable exception was the recent film "And Your Name is Jonah" which cast a Deaf child in the leading role.

As a result of the demonstration in San Francisco (which closed the theatre showing "Voices"), MGM agreed to make every effort to use Deaf actors to fill Deaf roles in future productions. MGM also agreed to use the National Association of the Deaf as a referral agency for this purpose as well as for technical assistance in films relating to deafness.

149

C. Dialogue

Pat

Pat₁: $\overline{\text{FUTURE   SATURDAY   #DO-DO}}^{\text{wh-q}}$

Pat₂: $\overset{\text{(gaze rt   )}}{\text{INDEX-}rt}$ **#CLUB   HAVE   MOVIE, $\overline{\text{ONE   DRAMA AGENT,}}^{\text{t}}$ SIGN**

Pat₃: **NOT-KNOW,   SATURDAY $\overset{\text{(gaze rt   )}}{\text{ME   (2h)alt.}me\text{-ASK-TO-}rt\text{"}spec\text{"}}$ SEE-SEE**

Pat₄: **RIGHT*,   #CO $\overset{\text{('trying to remember'}}{\underset{\textit{INDEX-rt} \longrightarrow}{\text{SOMETHING   BUY   TICKET}}}$ $\overset{\text{)puff.cheeks}}{\text{(2h)}company\text{-GIVE-TO-"}all\text{"}}$ nodding   FREE,**

   (gaze lf & rt   'guiltily'   )
   company-**GIVE-TO-"***each***"**

Pat₅: $\overset{\text{(gaze rt   )}}{\text{MAYBE   SATURDAY   NIGHT   MOVIE   DRAMA AGENT   DEAF}}$ $\overset{\text{brow raise}}{\text{INDEX-}rt}$

Pat₆: **"HAND-IT-OVER"**

Lee

                                                neg   wh-q

e_1: "DON'T-KNOW" (2h)NOT-KNOW (2h)NOT-YET DECIDE, (2h)WHY (2h)WHAT'S-UP (2h)"WHAT"

                                   q

e_2: OH-I-SEE, DEAF INDEX-*lf*

                                                  t

e_3: "THAT'S-RIGHT" REMEMBER AWHILE-AGO MOVIE, NAME ME FORGET, DOESN'T-MATTER

                     t   nodding   t

THAT-ONE INDEX-*lf*, DRAMA TWO DRAMA AGENT INDEX-*rt* SIGN, THOSE-TWO-*rt*,

HEARING

                    t   t

e_4: DEAF ALL-OVER, (2h)BECOME-ANGRY, LETTER,

(2h)alt.*"unspec"deaf people*-SEND-TO-*cntr* (2h)alt.COMPLAIN,

      t (body lean back   )

#CO, (2h)alt.*"unspec"deaf people*-SEND-TO-*me* "STAY-BACK" ENOUGH,

                                          (lean rt) (lean lf)   cond

DECIDE FROM-NOW-ON #IF MOVIE HAVE SIGN-*rt*, DEAF, "WELL",

WILL (2h)alt.ASK-TO-*"spec"* HIRE DEAF

                                 cond

e_5: ME DISBELIEVE ME, SUPPOSE DEAF,

                                               rapid nodding

ME ONE-DOLLAR DOLLAR *me*-PAY-OUT-TO-*"each"*

                                             ME

D. Key Illustrations

Pat

#DO-DO

NOT-KNOW

(2h)alt.*me*-ASK-TO-*"spec"*

Lee

OH-I-SEE

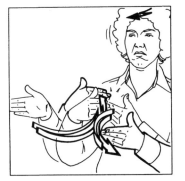

DOESN'T-MATTER

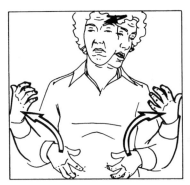

(2h)BECOME-ANGRY

(2h)alt.*"unspec"deaf people*-SEND-TO-*me*

FROM-NOW-ON

#IF

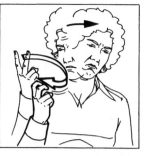

(2h)alt.ASK-TO-"spec"   **DISBELIEVE**   **me-PAY-OUT-TO-"each"**

E. Supplementary Illustrations

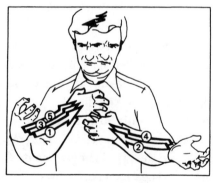

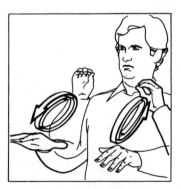

SEE-SEE   **GIVE-TO-"all"**   **GIVE-TO-"each"**

(2h)alt.COMPLAIN   **(2h)alt."unspec"deaf people-SEND-TO-cntr**

F. General Discussion: Distributional Aspect

The previous discussion of distributional aspect (Unit 9) focused on two verb modulations—the modulation that we write as *"all"* and the modulation called *"unspecified"* (abbreviated as *"unspec"*). In this discussion, we will introduce two more modulations which give information about how an action is distributed.

Recall that the *"all"* modulation indicates that the action happens to all of the people or things—like giving something to all of the people in the room or collecting all of the homework papers. Also remember that this modulation (and the other modulations) shows the spatial location of the people or things involved in the action. So, for example, if the people are all over the room, the arc movement will sweep across the signing space—as seen in the illustration below on the left. However, if the Signer is referring to a group of people located to the Signer's left, then the arc movement will include only that particular spatial location—as seen in the illustration on the right.

me-**ASK-TO**-*"all"*   *me*-**SHOW-TO**-*lf"all"*

Notice that the *"all"* modulation does not specify exactly how the distribution occurs. It doesn't tell you, for example, if the Signer 'asked' each person individually, or if the question was addressed to the group as a whole and anyone could answer. The *"all"* modulation is more general—like saying 'I asked them'.

If the Signer wants to specify that s/he individually asked each person in the group, then s/he will use the modulation that we write as *"each"*. This modulation also has an arc movement but the Signer repeats the regular movement of the verb while moving across the arc. The Signer's eyes and head tend to follow each repetition along the arc.

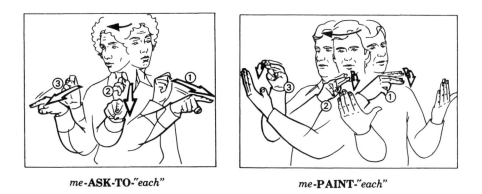

me-**ASK-TO**-"each"   me-**PAINT**-"each"

In the two illustrations above, the Signer is the subject, and the verb shows that the Signer does something to each member of a group individually. For example, the Signer may be asking each person in the room the same question one after the other; or the Signer may be re-painting each of the pictures on the wall. This modulation can also be used when the object is singular and it's the subject that is plural. For example, by moving the verb *from* different spatial locations in an arc, one could sign *"each"student*-**ASK-TO**-*me,* assuming that the students have been assigned a spatial location.

Recall that the *"unspecified"* or *"unspec"* modulation tells us that the same type of action occurs again and again, each time to or from a different individual or a different thing. However, this verb modulation does not focus on specific individuals or things—they remain un-specified. Accordingly, the Signer does not look at any specific locations in space but generally gazes and bobs his/her head from side to side while signing a verb with the *"unspec"* modulation—like *me*-**GIVE-TO**-*"unspec"* or, as illustrated in Unit 9, *police*-**ARREST**-*people"unspec"*.

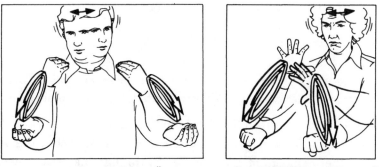

me-**GIVE-TO**-"unspec"   police-**ARREST**-people"unspec"

Notice that this modulation does not indicate that all of the people were given something or that the police arrested all of the people. Instead, the modulation indicates that 'some' or 'many' (depending on the speed and number of repetitions) people were given something or were arrested.

If the Signer wants to focus on the fact that s/he gave something to *specific* individuals within a group, s/he could use the modulation that we write as *"spec"* (referring to 'specified individuals').

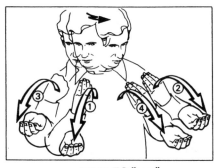

me-**GIVE-TO**-*"spec"*

Unlike the *"each"* modulation, the *"spec"* modulation indicates that the distribution of the action is *not* in serial order. That is, the *"spec"* modulation shows that the action happens with 'this one here' and then 'that one over there', etc. Another way that the *"spec"* modulation is different from the *"each"* modulation is that only 'some' or 'many' specific individuals are involved in the action—whereas the "each" modulation implies that action involves all of the individuals or things in the group. For example, if the Signer wants to describe the action (at a large Student Council meeting) of 'selecting various volunteers to help pass out papers', s/he would probably use the *"spec"* modulation, as illustrated below.

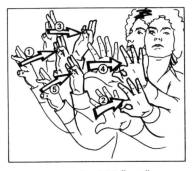

me-**SELECT**-*"spec"*

Thus far, we have described four different verb modulations—*"all"*, *"each"*, *"unspec"*, and *"spec"*. These modulations indicate: (a) simply that the action happened to all of the members of a group *("all")*, (b) that the action involved each individual or thing in an orderly manner *("each")*, (c) that the action involved many un-specified individuals or things over a period of time ("*unspec*"), or (d) that the action involved some/many specific individuals or things, in non-serial order. The Signer's decision to use a particular modulation depends on his/her perception of how the distribution actually occurred and whether s/he feels it is important or relevant to specify that actual distribution.

G. Text Analysis

Pat$_3$:
    (gaze rt   )
NOT-KNOW, SATURDAY ME (2h)alt.*me*-**ASK-TO**-*"spec"* **SEE-SEE**

- (2h)alt.*me*-**ASK-TO**-*"spec"*

  This is an example of a modulation which indicates how the action is distributed, as discussed above. The meaning the Signer wishes to convey is that s/he will ask certain people (not everyone) who, presumably, will know if the person signing in the movie is Deaf or not.

Lee$_3$:
                                                 t
"THAT-S-RIGHT" **REMEMBER** **AWHILE-AGO** **MOVIE,** **NAME** **ME** **FORGET,**
DOESN'T-MATTER,

                    t   nodding   t
THAT-ONE⁀INDEX-lf, **DRAMA** **TWO** **DRAMA⁀AGENT** **INDEX**-*rt* **SIGN,** **THOSE-TWO**-*rt*,

HEARING

- **NAME**

  In this context, this sign has the meaning 'title'. It is interesting to note that the sign **NAME** is often used by Deaf children when they want to know the fingerspelled English gloss for a sign.

- **DOESN'T-MATTER**

  This sign is often glossed as **ANYWAY** and it conveys the meanings 'it doesn't matter', 'doesn't make any difference', or 'anyway'.

- **THAT-ONE⁀INDEX**-*lf*

  This is an example of a definite pronoun. Here the pronoun refers to the movie. Notice also that this is another example of two signs used together in such a way that they look like a single sign.

- **THOSE-TWO**-*rt*

  This is another example of a pronoun. In this case, it refers to the two hearing actors. See Units 3 and 12 for a discussion of pronouns.

Pat$_4$:
                ('trying to remember'   )puff.cheeks nodding
RIGHT*, **#CO**   **SOMETHING** **BUY** **TICKET** (2h)*company*-**GIVE-TO**-*"all"* **FREE,**
              INDEX-*rt* ⟶

(gaze lf & rt 'guiltily'   )
    company-**GIVE-TO**-*"each"*

- **#CO**

  This is an example of a fingerspelled loan sign in ASL. In this case the loan is from the English abbreviation 'co.' for 'company'.

<u>   puff.cheeks</u>

- (2h)*company*-**GIVE-TO**-*"all"*

> This is an example of one of the modulations described in Unit 9 and reviewed in this unit. Notice how the *'puffed cheeks'* signal indicates that a large number of tickets were given away.

(gaze lf & rt 'guiltily'   )
-   *company*-**GIVE-TO**-*"each"*

> This is an example of one of the verb modulations described in this unit. Notice that the Signer first uses the *"all"* modulation to simply say that the company gave free tickets to all of the people. This modulation does not indicate how the distribution took place. Now the Signer uses the *"each"* modulation to show that the tickets were distributed one-by-one to each person.
>
> Also notice how the Signer's non-manual behaviors show that the company was embarrassed by the controversy and, thus, 'guiltily' gave out free tickets.

                  <u>   t   </u>   <u>   t   </u>

Lee$_4$: **DEAF ALL-OVER,** (2h)**BECOME-ANGRY, LETTER,**

(2h)alt.*"unspec"deaf people*-**SEND-TO**-*cntr* (2h)alt.**COMPLAIN,**

<u>   t   </u> (body lean back   )
#CO, (2h)alt.*"unspec"deaf people*-**SEND-TO**-*me* **"STAY-BACK" ENOUGH,**

                                             (lean rt) (lean lf)   cond
DECIDE FROM-NOW-ON #IF MOVIE HAVE SIGN-*rt,* **DEAF, "WELL",**

WILL (2h)alt.**ASK-TO**-*"spec"* **HIRE DEAF**

> - (2h)alt.*"unspec"deaf people*-**SEND-TO**-*cntr*
>
> > This is an example of the *"unspec"* modulation discussed in Unit 9 and reviewed in this unit. Notice that the subject is plural (Deaf people all over) and the object is singular (the company).
>
> (body lean back   )
> - (2h)alt.*"unspec"deaf people*-**SEND-TO**-*me* **"STAY-BACK" ENOUGH**
>
> > This is an excellent example of how a Signer will shift his/her body position and eye gaze in order to 'become' a particular character and directly quote that character. (See Unit 13 for further explanation). In this case, the Signer 'becomes' the company and then shows how the company responded to being flooded with letters. Notice that the change in the direction of movement of the verb ____-**SEND-TO**-____ clearly indicates that the Signer is now assuming the role of the company.

- $\overline{\text{\hspace{4cm}cond}}$
  #IF MOVIE HAVE SIGN-*rt*, DEAF, "WELL",

  This is an example of a condition in ASL. It occurs before the result or the consequence and, in this case, is introduced by the sign **#IF**. Unit 10 described two other signs that may be used to begin a conditional sentence— **SUPPOSE** and **#IF**wg. However, Signers can also sign conditional sentences without using **SUPPOSE, #IF,** or **#IF**wg because the non-manual *'cond'* signal also indicates that the sentence is a conditional.

- **WILL (2h)alt.ASK-TO-*"spec"* HIRE DEAF**

  This is the consequence or result that follows the condition described above. Notice that the *"spec"* modulation on the verb ____-**ASK-TO-**____ indicates that the company will ask specific individuals (presumably those that are qualified)—not everyone *("all")* or just anyone *("unspec")*.

Lee₅: **ME DISBELIEVE ME, SUPPOSE DEAF,** $\overline{\text{\hspace{2cm}cond}}$

   ME ONE-DOLLAR DOLLAR *me*-PAY-OUT-TO-*"each"* $\overline{\text{rapid nodding}}$
                                       ME

- $\overline{\text{\hspace{3cm}cond}}$
  SUPPOSE DEAF,

  This is another example of a condition in ASL. Notice that it begins differently than the one in Lee's previous turn. See Unit 10 for further discussion.

- **ME ONE-DOLLAR DOLLAR *me*-PAY-OUT-TO-*"each"***

  This is the result or the consequence of the condition. The sign **ONE-DOLLAR** is made with a twisting movement so that the palm moves from facing away from the Signer to facing toward the Signer. This movement can be used with the numbers 1-9 to express the meanings 'one dollar', 'two dollars', etc. Thus, Lee could have signed this segment without the sign **DOLLAR** since that meaning is already included in the sign **ONE-DOLLAR.**

  The sign *me*-**PAY-OUT-TO-*"each"*** has the modulation which means that the action will be distributed to each individual one-by-one.

H. Sample Drills

1. **NOT-KNOW, SATURDAY ME** (2h)alt.*me*-**ASK-TO-**"*spec*"

                                me-**GIVE-TO-**"*all*"

        (2h)alt.*me*-**SEND-TO-**"*unspec*"

                             me-**PAY-OUT-TO-**"*each*"

                             me-**GIVE-TO-**"*each*"

        (2h)alt.*me*-**SEND-TO-**"*spec*"

                             me-**PAY-OUT-TO-**"*all*"

                             me-**SEND-TO-**"*each*"

        (2h)alt.*me*-**ASK-TO-**"*unspec*"

        (2h)alt.*me*-**ASK-TO-**"*spec*"

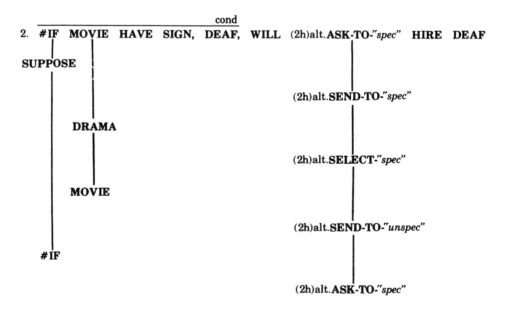

                                                  cond

2. **#IF MOVIE HAVE SIGN, DEAF, WILL** (2h)alt.**ASK-TO-**"*spec*" **HIRE DEAF**

SUPPOSE

                                           (2h)alt.**SEND-TO-**"*spec*"

        DRAMA

                                           (2h)alt.**SELECT-**"*spec*"

        MOVIE

                                           (2h)alt.**SEND-TO-**"*unspec*"

#IF

                                           (2h)alt.**ASK-TO-**"*spec*"

cond

3. ME   DISBELIEVE, SUPPOSE   DEAF,   ME   ONE-DOLLAR   *me*-PAY-OUT-TO-*"each"*

                                                             me-GIVE-TO-*"each"*

                                   HAPPEN

NOT-KNOW

                                            TWO-DOLLAR

                                                       me-GIVE-TO-*"spec"*

                  #IFwg

                               DEAF

DISBELIEVE

                                            ONE-DOLLAR

                                                       me-PAY-OUT-TO-*"each"*

                  SUPPOSE

I. Video Notes

If you have access to the videotape package designed to accompany these texts, you will notice the following:

- Notice Pat's facial and gaze behavior toward the end of his fourth turn—which shows the company's embarrassment Also notice the way he signs in a more 'stiff' manner while signing *company*-**GIVE-TO**-"*each*", also indicating the tensions aroused by the controversy and the company's guilty response.

- In Lee's fourth turn a particular non-manual signal occurs with the sign (2h)**BECOME-ANGRY.** This signal seems to convey the information that the action ('becoming angry') was both sudden and intense.

- Notice the body and gaze shift in the middle of Lee's fourth turn which indicates that she is "role playing" the company's reaction.

- Notice the non-manual signal '*cond*' in the one-shot of Lee's fourth and fifth turns and how the Signer's eye gaze and facial expression changes at the beginning of each 'result' segment.

- Notice how Lee rapidly nods her head at the end of her fifth turn to affirm her intention of giving each person a dollar if the actor is Deaf.

Video Package Notes:

If you have access to the videotape package designed to accompany these texts, you will see the following stories and narrative descriptions which appear after dialogues 10-18.

Don't Sign With Your Hands Full—M.J. Bienvenu
   Notice how the Signer repeatedly shifts her body position, facial expression, and eye gaze to "role play" the giant and the little girl. Notice also how this joke requires some understanding of Sign Language and the Deaf Community.

The Roadrunner Wins Again—Ella Mae Lentz
   This "cartoon" is told almost entirely with classifiers. Notice how the Signer locates the roadrunner to her right and the coyote to her left in the very beginning of the narrative and then uses these locations to describe the actions of each character.

Football Fantasy—Gilbert C. Eastman
   Notice the many different classifier handshapes used to describe the stadium, the 'fans', and the actual football game. Notice also how the Signer rapidly changes "perspective" (e.g. from the player kicking the ball—to the ball flying upwards—to the fans watching the ball—to the ball falling down—to the player catching it) to add excitement to the story and make it 'come alive' for the viewer.

Think Big—Pat Graybill
   Notice the classifier handshapes used in this joke. Again, notice how the Signer frequently changes perspective while telling the story and how the Signer's whole body changes when he becomes the main character. Finally, notice how the Signer shows the cockiness of the main character toward the end of the story.

The Race: A to Z—M.J. Bienvenu
   This entire story is told using the handshapes from the manual alphabet. Each handshape is used as the handshape for a specific sign, and the story is told "in alphabetical order". "Alphabet stories" such as this one are often told at parties.

Earliest Memories—Nathie Couthen
   This is a true description of the Signer's earliest memories after becoming deaf. Notice how the Signer's body shifts back when she describes herself lying in bed. Notice also how she describes the talking and laughter which she cannot hear.

The Candy Caper—M.J. Bienvenu
   Notice how the Signer changes her signing when she "becomes" the little girl in the story. By shifting her position, facial expression, and eye gaze, the Signer clearly indicates when an adult is talking as opposed to when the little girl is talking.

Somethin's Fishy—Larry Berke
   Notice how the Signer uses classifiers to show the spatial (locative) relationships between various things. Notice also how the Signer "stays in character" while describing how excited the little boy became when he thought he had caught a trout.

INDEX OF ILLUSTRATIONS

The following is a list of all of the sign illustrations in this text. The illustrations for each unit are listed alphabetically according to their glosses. In cases where the illustration appears in more than one unit, those units are listed on the right.

Unit 10

Unit 11

_____ intense
DISTANT-FUTURE

_____ puff.cheeks
DISTANT-FUTURE

EVERY-DAY . . . 13

EVERY-MONDAY

EVERY-MORNING . . . 12

EVERY-NIGHT

EVERY-OTHER-MONDAY

EVERY-THREE-WEEK

EVERY-WEEK

EVERY-YEAR

FROM-NOW-ON . . . 18

NOW

REMEMBER . . . 15

SAME-OLD-THING . . . 17

SOMETIME-IN-THE-AFTERNOON

SOMETIME-IN-THE-MORNING

THEREABOUTS . . . 15

THINK⌢SAME-AS

TWO-WEEK-PAST

"UMMM"

UP-TILL-NOW

USE-ASL"regularly"

VARIOUS-THINGS

#WHAT

WORK"long time"

Unit 12

CAPTION

DOESN'T-MATTER . . . 18

DON'T-CARE

EVERY-MORNING . . . 11

GO-rt . . . 15, 17

GO-TO-rt . . . 10

INTERPRET . . . 16

KNOW+

me-**LOOK-AT-**lf & rt⟵⟶

MOVIE

NOT-KNOW . . . 15, 18

NOT-LIKE . . . 17

NOT-WANT . . . 14

OURSELVES

QMwg . . . 10

THAT-ONE-rt

THAT-ONE*-rt

THAT-ONE⌢INDEX-rt . . . 15

THINK⌢YOURSELF

US-THREE

US-THREE-rt

US-TWO

WE (referents not present)

WE (referents present)

WHY⌢NOT . . . 17

YOU-THREE

YOUR (plural)

YOURSELVES-AND-MYSELF

Unit 13

me-**AGREE-WITH-**you

you-**AGREE-WITH-**"each other"

ITS-NOTHING

me-**LOOK-AT-**teachers"overtime" . . . 17

Unit 14

me-**PITY**-*you*

(2h)alt.**PUT**-*trophies*-**IN**-*box*

STATE-SCHOOL . . . 15

STRUGGLE*"regularly"*

(2h)alt.**TAKE-DOWN**-*pictures*

TIME⁀THREE

TROPHY

WHAT'S-UP . . . 10

(2h)alt.**A-CL**

(2h)**A-CL***"in a row"*

(2h)**A-CL***"in rows"*

(2h)**A-CL***"sweep in a row"*

(2h)**A-CL***"sweep in a row"*

(2h)**C-CL**'small group'

(2h)**C-CL**'large group'

(2h)alt.**C-CL**'pictures on wall'

V:-CL*@rt,out* } 'sit facing each other'
V:-CL *@rt,in*

Unit 15

AGE-SEVEN-*rt*   **AGE-THREE**-*lf*

DEAF . . . 10

#DO-DO . . . 13, 18

FRECKLES-ON-*face*

GO-*rt* . . . 12, 17

HEARING . . . 10

#JOB . . . 10

NOT-KNOW . . . 12, 18

OH-I-SEE . . . 18

REMEMBER . . . 11

STATE-SCHOOL . . . 14

THAT-ONE⁀INDEX-*rt* . . . 12

"THAT'S-RIGHT"

THEREABOUTS . . . 11

"WHAT"

1-CL-*cntr*'ski down hill'

(2h)**4→CL**-*lf*'fence on side of hill'

5:↓-CL*@rt*'state school'

5:↓-CL*@rt*'school'
B-CL'road near school'

5:↓-CL*@rt*'school'
INDEX-*rt*'near school'

5:↓-CL*@rt*'school'
NOT-MUCH

V-CL-*cntr*'stand atop hill'
B↓-CL-*cntr*'hill'

(2h)**B**outline-**CL**-*cntr*'hill'

Unit 16

ALTOGETHER

ASSEMBLE-TO-*cntr* . . . 10

ASSEMBLE-TO-*rt*

CAMERA-RECORD-*arc*

DIFFERENT+++-*arc* . . . 10, 11

FEW

(2h)**GROUP-MARCH-TO**-*rt*

INTERPRET . . . 12

KNOW-NOTHING

KNOW-THAT

me-**LOOK-AT**-*interpreters"each"*

NARRATE

NOT*

PEA-BRAIN*

Unit 17

Unit 18